My Father's Places

My Father's Places

A Portrait of Childhood by
Dylan Thomas' Daughter

Aeronwy Thomas

Constable · London

Constable & Robinson Ltd
3 The Lanchesters
162 Fulham Palace Road
London W6 9ER
www.constablerobinson.com

First published in the UK by Constable,
an imprint of Constable & Robinson, 2009

Extracts from letters taken from *Dylan Thomas:
The Collected Letters*, edited by Paul Ferris,
published by J.M. Dent, 1985.

A copy of the British Library Cataloguing in Publication
Data is available from the British Library

ISBN   978-1-84901-005-4

Printed and bound in the EU

1 3 5 7 9 10 8 6 4 2

Mixed Sources
Product group from well-managed
forests and other controlled sources
www.fsc.org Cert no. SA-COC-1565
© 1996 Forest Stewardship Council
FSC

To Huw, Hannah and Oscar

Arriving, 1949

Dylan before Laugharne, with Aeron and an unknown man in front of the greenhouse. (Photo courtesy of Reg Evans).

We were met at Carmarthen station by Billy Williams of the Williams family who owned and ran the electric generator, the buses, taxis and garage at Laugharne as well as the Brown's Hotel. My father, Dylan, my mother, Caitlin, and I piled in to his family taxi with our higgledy-piggledy set of suitcases and belongings. Basic furniture from the Manor House, mainly given by Maggs (my father's patron, Margaret Taylor) and well-wishers, was being sent separately while Mother was forced to leave behind my cradle, her round table and the magnificent double bed from the Chelsea studio.

The taxi took us along the cliffwalk to the path that led to Cliff House. At the top of the path, by an old iron gate, a clump of daisies radiated their whiteness and, although we were driving past, time seemed to stop. I can remember arriving on that first day, carrying our bags and hand-held belongings, toiling down the path from the walk above the Boat House. The pathway to the Boat House was too narrow for a car so we carried our bags over the uneven surface while we looked over the low cliff wall at the sand and water beyond. The overhanging bushes and hanging plants clung to the cliff-face like festoons waving a greeting. We walked, laden with bags and books, along the last stretch of the path, rough and natural under our feet, to our new home, a three-storeyed cottage called the Boat House.

It looked heavenly: a place to explore, to run around, where we would be living forever. It had verandas and balconies, water-butts, stepped gardens, a large boat shed in the back yard, the harbour and a wall protecting us from the wilds of the friendly estuary beyond. We

The Boat House. (Photo courtesy of Colin Shrewing).

had fallen upon paradise. As we were settling in, my father wrote to Margaret Taylor, who had arranged for the place, that, 'this is it: the place, the house, the workroom, the time' and that he could never thank her enough. 'I shall write in this water and tree room on the cliff, every word, will be my thanks to you . . .'

In my memory it hardly ever rained that season. From the balcony that ran round the cottage like a midriff, on two sides of the house, I looked at the river estuary and beyond the view of Laugharne. There was sun on the water and rivulets threaded their way through drifts of sandbanks and tidal flats away from the coast with its mudflats, channels and moored fishing boats under the castle walls, and the square and hill where my mother and father used to live in the thirties in a small fisherman's cottage called Eros. On the crest of the hill was the council estate of Orchard Park. There was sun on the water. Straight away, Mother found a 'mother's help' in the village: a young woman called Dolly Long. When I knew Dolly she must have been in her twenties, with a stock of floral, Vera Lynn dresses. She wore her black hair long and lank over her narrow shoulders; her face was thin and stricken. She was, after my mother and of course Granny, the most beautiful, radiant person I ever knew. She belonged to our child's world more than to Mother's world, warning us whenever anyone descended to our kitchen haunts with, 'Now we're for it!'

Dolly soon had an array of faces for Booda, a fixture in the kitchen. He was what was termed then as 'deaf and dumb', though the noise he made when trying to express himself with gestures and movements was impressive. Yet as children we never once mimicked Booda; he was one of us, part of the underworld away from the proper adults upstairs.

3

He was our nearest neighbour and lived in the Ferry House, a house built on a rock at sea level. He was the survivor of three brothers, the Roberts, who ferried passengers between Laugharne and the Llangain peninsula. The other two had died. We could see the bell house just across the water which you rang when you wanted a ride. Poor Booda did not hear any of these calls and only occasionally took in his boat those people who caught his attention outside his house.

The Lawn

On the Lawn: Dolly and Llewelyn in the foreground.

We had arrived in May and by the summer it was possible to bathe on the mud and sandbanks when the tide was out. We would pack up sandwiches, chocolate, hankies, thermoses, towels and

Mother's tobacco tins into an open wicker basket and visit the nearby 'lawn' – a patch of grass beside the sea about five minutes walk along the shore. Mably, our dog, would join us uninvited for our walk. He had belonged to Granny and Grandpa Thomas originally, rescued from their former home at Blaencwm, but knew where his loyalties lay. This transfer was confirmed by a change in the dog's name; Mably Owen was a friend of my parents and probably not known to my grandparents. He took to his new identity immediately, abandoning his first owners and moving to the Boat House, where there was no time to become bored and always someone swimming, walking or cycling with a dog for company. Mother and I walked past the Ferry House along the coastal shore at low tide towards the lawn, clambering across boulders and slipping on mud in sandals and plimsolls. We used the seaweed carpet draped over the stones to walk over the slippery mud, stretching our legs from rock to rock. Mably took his own route, crying when his calloused paw hit a stone under the mud.

Beside the lawn there was what looked like a tiny, ruined chapel, with only three of its walls in place, where we would sit to take our clothes off and put on our swimsuits ready for a dip. When Mother realized that no one ever visited the lawn except us, she used to slip off her suit to swim with nothing on. I would object loudly, imagining eyes peering from all the bushes growing across the cliff-face. The lawn, built on an elevated ledge surrounded by a curving, crescent-moon-shape wall, was bare of any shrubbery. On emerging from the water, my swimsuit weighed me down so that I bagged like a small bloated whale. Mother would rush to the chapel, dive into the basket, emerging with chocolate before remembering to cover herself with a threadbare towel. Afterwards, I had to dry her back. Damp but fortified, we would climb over the lawn edge to sit squat-legged, eat our sandwiches and drink black tea. Mother would place the baccy tin between her knees and select strands of tobacco to roll a cigarette with one hand against her hip.

It was here that she told me the history of the place. It was called Faulkner's Lawn after the grand family, part of the 'crach' (the word in Welsh to describe the snobs or gentry), who lived nearby and built it as a tennis court in the early 1900s. A steep cliff path linked the 'lawn' to the cliff-top house of Glan-y-mor. She also told me the path leading from Faulkner's Lawn up the hill to the grand house at the top was called Gin Lane. Smugglers brought in gin during the nineteenth century to sell to the gentry. The path from the estuary crossing our front door and leading up in the same direction was another 'gin lane'. Contraband was frequently deposited at the Boat House wall. Under the flagstones by the door there was an empty passageway that might have been very useful.

As time went on that summer we began to meet more people and our jaunts to the lawn grew more crowded; the locals were not interested in swimming, but instead we played games: catch, hide-and-seek (in the lawn sides and chapel) and rounders. My older brother Llewelyn first disdained joining us on our outings. He was three years older and at nine years old already knew everything. My mother called him 'The Bible'; his knowledge of birds, marine animals and children's literature was already immense, especially by my standards. He was also not interested in swimming in the estuary, preferring the open sea and sands of Pendine, a few miles by bus.

When he came with us to the lawn he often invited some of his new friends for boisterous games, with him in charge. They were

David Richards, son of Phillip Richards of the Cross House, and David's cousin, Phil, a slight, nervous boy similar in temperament to my brother but not bossy. Other boys, Clement (Clem) and David Evans, were also invited but I was not pleased because they left me out of their jaunts. Llewelyn organized games of cricket, in which I could participate by picking up the ball. When I objected he told me to shut up and do what I was told. Mother said to let me have a turn which caused scuffles and disagreements. The boys agreed with Llewelyn that I was best left on the sidelines.

On one occasion, Dolly was there and said out of Llewelyn's hearing that he was an awful bully but I found myself excusing my brother, who knew when I was behaving badly or angling for attention. At the Boat House, Dolly used to defend me openly against everyone, including Mother. It was either Dolly's mother or mine who said, 'Dolly won't hear a word against you.' The expression was dangerously close to a cliché, I noted with satisfaction. 'Keep off of her,' Dolly warned Llewelyn when the verbal battles we had from time-to-time turned physical. In some terrible way, he was only meting out divine justice with a well-aimed blow or word.

But he could also be the nicest person in the world, however fickle. I appreciated his kindness and inventiveness. One day, Llewelyn suggested taking our boat to the lawn; an idea that had never occurred to us before. It must have been after my younger brother's birth that first summer when he was given a rowing boat called the Cuckoo. Of course, even though it was Colm's boat everyone used it except him as he was only a baby. Dolly and Booda warned us about a whirlpool somewhere near the Ferry House between the house and the lawn. A local man, Donald Raye, later told me how many cocklers 'drownded at high tide' on these same mudflats. In one family, the daughter Olive died in the whirlpool when caught swimming at turn of tide, and in a separate incident her brother drowned when fishing. Three boys in a makeshift boat were also 'drownded'. The drowned girl's ashes and, later, flowers at anniversaries, were strewn at the site of the whirlpool.

My Father at Work

That first short summer was a particularly happy one before I was sent to the Laugharne primary school, and before the visitors from London and America knew we were there. Father was working every afternoon on 'Over Sir John's Hill', his word-picture of the hill he saw from the shed, while Mother was still arranging the furniture in the Boat House and painting the woodwork. Like Mother's personal dress sense, her choice of colours worked, or so Margaret Taylor said. Margaret's taste was more floral, covering her walls at Oxford with Sanderson William Morris-style wallpaper, but she appreciated the daring colour choices Mother made in dress and decorating.

My father had decided to turn his attention to poetry, his first love. He would concentrate on 'his own work,' he said in a letter to Frances Hughes, 'cutting out all time-wasting broadcasts, articles, useless London visits'. For a while his determination held and he turned down one talk for the BBC because it would take too long to prepare, and asked his agent to cancel or postpone his agreement to adapt Henrik Ibsen's *Peer Gynt* for radio. But London still beckoned and soon he was asking his producer Hector MacIver to suggest a date to meet and to arrange a job for him in London to cover his expenses. In October, he was apologizing to John Davenport, with whom he wrote the novel *The Death of the King's Canary*, that he saw so little of him on his last London visit, and foresaw another: 'I may be up in a fortnight and will write, ring or just glaze in.' In another letter, he was sorry to miss him when he was up 'in the smoke last week'.

There were also commissions closer to home which forced him to go to Swansea. It would have been difficult for him to refuse such an occasion to spend time with some of his old friends, the drinkers of cherry 'dashes' at the Kardomah café in the halcyon, hopeful days of young manhood – Vernon Watkins, Fred Janes, John Pritchard and Dan Jones. Together with a shifting band of composers, writers, paint-ers and others, who included Charlie Fisher and Tom Warner, they were a loose-knit community of artists meeting for talk and stimulus. The café where they met on the second floor dated back to Edwardian times. According to Mother, those early friendships made by my father in Swansea, and cultivated at the Kardomah, were to remain with him all his life; lifelong friends who all turned up at his funeral.

At home, however, finances were worse than before with so much of my father's income docked by the taxman at source. He used the birth of my baby brother Colm on 24 July 1949 as his chief argument in begging letters of this time. He was writing jocularly enough before the birth, to Hector MacIver: 'My wife is just about to go to the infir-mary to have a Thomas. There are not enough of them already.'

My mother could not bear him demeaning himself by begging and said so with no effect. In his shed, however, he could write what he liked. He wrote to many friends, including John Davenport, about their poverty. He pointed to the bills, to the cessation of coal deliveries and the threat to the milk, 'essential things in a baby-packed, freezing house. I'm summonsed for rates. No more meat.' He was 'literally without one shilling' and – ludicrous climax – there was no money for 'sweets for Aeron'. Penniless, nonetheless he joined another London club, the Savage, in March 1949, and at least five cheques were returned from there. In the meantime, his two-year membership of the National Liberal Club, most inappropriate for a socialist, finished – he renamed it the National Lavatory Club due to the imposing and palatial WCs there.

Colm's arrival was added to my father's excuses for failing to deliver contracted scripts and the letters continued in their inventive vein. For Princess Marguerite Caetani, who ran a literary magazine from her Rome palazzo and published his work from time to time, he produced a list which he called his 'sea of sorries'. He never seemed to appreciate the rule that one excuse is better than two. Not sending a promised poem to John Davenport for *Arena*, he used his Swansea script as the reason in what he called 'a scruffy note from a scruffy man', a typical self-deprecation which may have helped his case.

My father did find time, however, to read to me once or twice a week, usually on bath night. He was usually kind when he bumped into me, shouted sometimes (but usually asked Mother to do the shouting if I made too much noise), and only once or twice passed on the street without recognizing me. Once when I was asked to collect him from the Brown's Hotel when he was late for lunch, we passed each other on Victoria Street near the bakery before I saw and claimed him as my own.

'Mummy's cross with you,' I told him.

'Uh-huh,' he said, looking through me.

'Very cross,' I said to gain his attention.

He looked up, more interested.

'Well, not very cross,' I reverted to the truth.

We walked along comfortably and admired the scenery without a word. 'I found him,' I announced to Mother as he shambled behind. He couldn't negotiate the path down to the front door as nimbly as I could, and I ran ahead to show him how. 'Good girl,' said Mother, ruffling my curls with her one free hand, the other occupied with holding Colm.

Once he had made it down the path, my father beamed at the baby. What? Even my father favours him, I thought to myself. Well, he was quite endearing, my better-self said. But I'd have to punish him sometime for being the favourite, I resolved.

Colm's Arrival

When Mother first arrived back from the infirmary in Billy's taxi she got out at Brown's to show off Colm. There was a throng of sightseers to wish her well, pry at the baby, counting his fingers and toes; they looked and prodded, and all was well. Dad and I stood at the edge of the welcoming crowd. He gently pushed me forward to be greeted by Mother and I was waiting for her face to light up with love on seeing me but she was too occupied. After waiting, I returned to Dad who took my hand.

'Cat,' he said over the tumult, 'I'm taking Aeron back to the house and we'll wait at the top of the walk . . . is that all right?'

Only then did she ask, 'Where's Aeron? She must see the baby.'

But I certainly did not wish to see the interloper and felt the tears

Colm's arrival. (Photo courtesy of Rollie McKenna).

welling up in my eyes. Colm, wrapped up like a papoose, was unaware of the pain he was causing.

'Let's go', I said to Dad, trying hard to sound normal, turning my head away as we walked up Victoria Street so that he wouldn't see the tears streaming down my face, my shoulders heaving. He patted me on the back as he'd seen Mother do a hundred times but it wasn't the same. I loved him for trying. As we passed the cemetery along the cliff-side and Dad looked out towards the sea, I wiped my sodden face on the sleeve of my cardigan and tried to regulate my step with his; after all, we were both outsiders now Colm was here.

A few months later, Colm's head was covered with blond fluff, soon to become tight curls, and he smiled with blue, blue eyes. To my disgust, he smiled most of the time unless he had a dirty nappy or was hungry and everyone loved him. He was hard to resist, though I was trying hard. His full name was Colm Garan Thomas, of all silly names. Colm was Irish, Mother told me, and Garan meant heron in Welsh. That seemed better than my second name, Bryn, but perhaps being called after a bird that stood for hours on one leg was worse than a hill, both of which we saw every day. I often thought deeply on these matters, without answers, and resolved to ask someone what they thought. Now, who would be a good person, I pondered, and considered Granny, who still loved me best whatever I was called. My first name had originated because I was conceived in the Aeron Valley near the River Aeron – in 1942, during the war years, my parents had escaped the bombs by staying at a friend's farm, Plas Gelli, in New Quay. My mother returned there in 1944, with me as a baby, leaving my father in London working for the Ministry of Information as a script writer.

I was delighted when, a few weeks after Colm's birth, Mother asked if I would like to go cockle gathering. Now that was something a baby couldn't do. Mother was fascinated by the cockle gatherers, women from Laugharne and Ferryside who trawled the sands at the extreme point of the estuary called the Ginst, under Sir John's Hill, loading their panniered donkeys with cockles. Colm was left with Dolly and we took our bucket and a small spade to collect cockles for the family. Mother would fry them and add enough garlic and pepper to make us sneeze; Dolly would douse them in malt vinegar.

The cocklers ignored us, after a nod, not considering us a threat to their livelihood. They dug with a proper spade, then sifted the sand with a riddle, transferring the cockles to a hessian sack tied round their waists. At the incoming tide, the cockles were loaded on boats for washing; some of the cocklers had tanks at the back of their homes or used a communal washer with a stream and hand-pump at nearby Fernhill.

We all bent to our tasks; Mother and I scrabbled and dug in the wet sand in search of shells. I dug for them by feel, not relying on sight, as they were sea-washed to a sand colour, their shells corrugated like the tin over our outside loo. Mother was pleased with me and said I would soon learn to tread fish without throwing them back. She told me that the cockles were cleaned and sorted by local women in the cockle factory on the Grist to be pickled in jars, and others sold fresh in the markets of Carmarthen and Swansea. Ours were soaked over-night in a bucket outside the kitchen door to clear off the sand.

I fell asleep worried about the cockle donkeys standing patiently all day on the sand. Mother reassured me the cockle women loved their donkeys more than their husbands and would tuck them up at night with blankets to keep out the damp. Once there were many more, she told me, left to graze on what was called the Green Banks, the lower end of town by the water.

That summer a christening was arranged. Augustus John, Vernon Watkins, Dan Jones, and Ebi and Ivy Williams from the Brown's Hotel and their family were all there. But Colm was missing and Mother was sure she had brought him in the pram. An American professor drawled, 'Well, we'd better look for him.' I fiddled with the gold ring he had given me for a christening present and kept my distance, determined to tell my mother if he came too near me again.

My brother Colm, less than a month old, was being christened at St Martin's Church, Laugharne, and I was included in the ceremony as an afterthought: Aeron Hart Thomas (although I am Aeronwy Bryn Thomas according to my birth certificate). It was 12 August 1949 and I was six. The godparents, Elisabeth Lutyens for me and Ivy Williams, Helen and Bill McAlpine for my brother, stood by the church door, sad yews dripping water on their heads. There was a flurry of agitation among the assembled group, most of whom had travelled from Swansea or further.

The vicar announced triumphantly that he had found Colm in a bundle of blankets behind an ancient headstone. I feigned surprise but my parents knew the culprit. I ran to Dad from Mum, who had the baby in her arms.

'He wasn't far, was he? Someone was bound to find him,' said Dad. 'Are you nervous?' I thought he meant at Mother's anger, and shuffled my shoes, not answering. 'About the christening?' he said, making it plain. I had nearly forgotten the occasion was not just for the gilded baby boy.

'No, so long as you hold my hand,' I said, outmanoeuvring the guests who would want to monopolize him.

'All right, silly,' he said, ruffling my curls and allowing himself to be blackmailed. 'Now, don't worry,' he said, as we filed into church, the vicar guiding us.

We celebrated the two baptisms back in the Boat House. It took ten minutes to walk the street route from the church past the pub and the bakery, along the rough cliff-side walk. The steep incline down to the Boat House made it difficult to navigate the pram, people and crates of beer to the final obstacle, a step by the front door. The party began upstairs in the sitting room on the same level as the entrance, and moved downstairs, by a rope handrail, to the lower storey and our dining room. Drinks were handed round, some in cups because there weren't enough glasses. Colm smiled beatifically; he had a knack of charming people even at one month old. I wouldn't join the Colm worshippers and intended to hide him again until they forgot him forever, but it was difficult to plot my revenge when he directed the torchbeam of his morning smile at me from his cot in the room we shared.

The party got louder. 'Burlington Bertie from Bow' was one of the songs I can remember and Mother donned her tulle and velvet dancing skirts, and started to embarrass me, leaping on to the dining room table to swirl and cavort. I retreated into a corner where Dad stood looking round like a benevolent teddy bear, talking to Augustus and drinking beer from one of Granny's best porcelain cups. From his vast height Augustus bent down to ask kindly if I wanted something . . . a drink perhaps. I showed him my ring and told him I only drank cider in the kitchen.

'Who gave you that?' they both wanted to know.

I helpfully poured more beer from the bottle which was making dark rings on the desk instead of answering. Dad respected my silence, smiled sweetly with his broken teeth, and patted my head again, to show Augustus I wasn't so bad. With Colm around I would have to rely on Dad for attention and was going to be on my best behaviour and never have tantrums again.

After midnight, everyone left except for one or two out for the count on the floor – debris to be cleared in the morning. I watched from my bedroom window as the departing guests crawled up the moonlit path on their knees. Whenever people had been drinking at our house, they were warned of the dangers of falling over the edge on to the cliff-face and mud rocks, and the regulars automatically crawled or walked four-pawed up the path to the cliffwalk. In the morning, it was the clearest of days and I wandered on to the balcony. The bodies on the floor began to stir and one had the temerity to open the sitting room door on to the balcony, the children's' domain. I told him it was unsafe and he scuttled back indoors.

The dining room at the Boat House.

It was soon late summer but the sun still shone in my memory. When Mother was not moving about, she loved to lie in the sun. One day she was chatting to a friend, Mary Keene, lying on coats in the back garden. Mary was half undressed but kept her trousers on as she only had one leg but Mother had taken off her bra and rolled her knickers down. I was nervous that someone would see them so I joined Dolly who was beating clothes to a pulp against a washing board at the kitchen sink. There were more clothes and towels in a cockle bucket and even more grey garments were being boiled in a cooking pot. I watched the pillowslips being cooked on the Aga as the brown scum and accompanying cream colour bubbles rose to the surface.

'Is that all dirt?' I wanted to know. She added what looked like a piece of rag to the clothes' stew, laughed, and said it was a sachet called Dolly Blue. The blue powder turned everything white. In another large pan which often cooked potatoes and spaghetti, water boiled for the sink wash. The steam rose and you could hardly see out of the kitchen window. Dolly took a stick with a wedge on the end and stirred the mess of navy knickers in the bucket. There were only a couple (a week's worth) but they were large. She took one out of the bucket and smeared hard green soap against the intimate bits, rubbing the cloth against the board.

Dolly's hands always turned a raw red on wash day. She complained that she had two washing days every week because she had her home wash to do as well as ours but at least she had a copper and a mangle. When clothes couldn't be dried outside they were draped on fireguards where they cooked and steamed, drying before a lit open fire in the dining room. Hard-to-dry articles like my lisle panties or towels were hung over the rods in front of the Aga.

One day Mary Keene's daughter, Alice, came to visit. She was my age but I was in charge as my mother and Mary chatted round the wooden table on the scruffy veranda, drinking tea and smoking. We walked to the end of the cliffwalk where Alice admired the collapsed houses.

'The cliff-side gave way,' I stated melodramatically but truthfully. 'It might fall on the Boat House any time.'

'What would you save?' asked Alice.

I had to think for a few seconds before I conceded it would be Colm, and not my books.

Booda appeared and waved to us in a friendly way.

'He's all right,' I assured Alice. 'He understands anything you say but you have to pretend you're in a play.'

I asked if Dolly was still washing by bending over an imaginary board and beating imaginary clothes. He nodded and indicated he was going back to his house with the damp twigs, tipping his cap at us both. Alice nodded in acknowledgement. She would soon find her own way of communicating with Booda.

I took her down a path to the waterside to see the ruined chapel and the lawn. We pretended to play the organ and started to sing hymns. She didn't know the ones in Welsh, which was a relief as I only knew the first line or so. So we moved on to collecting china and shells in the mud, taking our plimsolls off to slide from one likely area of mud to another, sometimes falling. Alice looked a little worried at first until I told her that the mud would dry and Dolly would brush it off.

When the tide started to turn, I said we had to run home or we'd be cut off and have to swim through the whirlpool not far from the Ferry House. We ran home, but when we got there we found the women were chatting. Gathering clouds and a fresh wind made them drape cardigans over their shoulders. Luckily, the tide came in and they retreated to the house, though the water in the garden never reached the wooden table where they had been sitting.

Shortly after, we could see Mary Keene leaving, walking regally up the path, her wooden leg stiff but functional, the good leg taking most of the weight. She was very tall and beautiful and reputedly a model in London. But Alice stayed with me and we became firm friends. Later we must have done something more than ordinarily dreadful because Mother beat us both on our bare bottoms with the back of a hairbrush.

Dolly, a pile of half-dry clothes on her arm, said that was enough, Mrs Dylan. Alice could not go home because she couldn't sit down. She cried intermittently as we looked forlornly through the window at the soft rain and the full tide flooding the garden. The washing was draped everywhere and Dolly was debating whether to light a fire. Mother had ruined all the excitement of taking Alice round the best landmarks and my world was all water. I rubbed my behind and practised sitting down. It wasn't comfortable yet, Alice and I agreed. But I was beginning to forget the beating and Alice agreed that the flooding tide in the back garden was exciting, which I accepted as a compliment to me and the Boat House.

Forgetting our ordeal, I planned with Alice what we would do on her next visit. I would show her the secret rat holes and the farm at the end of the cliffwalk with the tethered, barking dog and the sheep grazing on the slopes, so steep in parts you wondered why they didn't fall off. I did not usually venture past the stile into the fields belonging to the farm but Alice made me feel bolder. By the time I'd hinted at the thrills and horrors that might befall one past the stile we quite forgot the unpleasantness with Mother.

Nearer home, I would show her the rubbish which was thrown over the wall to float away to Swansea at turn of tide and the ribs of a long-lost boat stuck in the mud which could only be seen at low tide and was not to be approached. We stood in wonder to watch Mother diving off the wall into the tide, though we tried to ignore her.

My father was away in London again and Mother was grumbling. He had promised to stay in Laugharne and work on poems, but he sought any pretext to escape. He accepted six broadcasts in London and two in Wales. In addition, after much organization, with help from James Laughlin, Margaret Taylor and David Higham, he was about to leave Laugharne for his longest jaunt ever, four months travel and reading in America and Canada. Before the three next American tours my mother objected loudly to what she called their madness, but I was not aware of her making any objection to this first American trip.

With Father away, the Boat House filled with children: Llewelyn and I, Dolly's son and niece, and our Laugharne school friends. We'd climb on the rail and the square wooden water butt, and jump on to the corrugated-iron roof of the outside lavatory and the branches of a large elderberry bush. We'd gallop up the central stairs of the house, hoisting ourselves with the nautical twisted rope hand rail, then out through the front door to the balcony, stopping to gather breath and glance at the estuary, smooth and untroubled.

We knew every step and run of the place and respected the dangers. Sometimes our games grew savage and girls turned on boys. Llewelyn was head of the gang and hated to be disobeyed so my little friend Shelagh and I would taunt him with the song he most hated, 'Silent Night', with our 'silent' rising in a provocative wail. On a later occasion, he would take his revenge on our taunting by dropping my doll's house over the cliff. We watched it shatter and imagined what it must be like for a human being to go over.

The estuary, with tern, gull and heron, and its surrounding country-side, with hawk and sparrow, was our extended garden. Standing on the balcony or the veranda below, we could watch the water slowly rising in a moon-shaped pool as it seeped from an opening in the wall which we called 'the harbour'. We kept our boat, the Cuckoo, under the veranda, beside a large shed. There was a rubber dinghy left permanently blown up, and planks for floating in the pool at full tide. As the water subsided we collected the tall forked sticks of shorn branches used for holding up the washing line, blown-up ducks and forgotten towels floating or half-immersed in the water or retrieved those wedged in the harbour before they floated into the big sea beyond.

Down the estuary.

My father described the Boat House as: 'his house on stilts high among beaks and palavers of birds' in 'Poem on his Birthday'. Stilts or long poles supported the wooden projections of the veranda and his working shed on the cliffwalk. On the veranda was the weather-beaten kitchen table and chairs. When the weather was mild enough the grown-ups sat there, feet on chairs, to smoke or drink tea, now and again throwing a glance at the water. When she sat rolling a cigarette, sitting on the table with a cup of tea, Mother would never call us back.

We children were always too busy to sit for long. We preferred running along the balcony or the veranda and along the wall, crusted with lichen, rough grass and pinks. We used the garden wall as a short cut to the rocks which lay at the end of the garden, wavy steps hewn by the wind and water. We would run jumping from one flat rock to another, scrambling along the rougher reaches, cloven-hooved in our black plimsolls. We would bound up the narrow steps to the cliffwalk above my father's shed, to Laugharne beyond.

We often went to the square called the Grist below the castle, with a market cross, bus-stop and water pump, I would look back to see if the Boat House was still there, and its whitewashed neighbour, the Ferry House. To my fond eye, the Boat House looked out in all directions, its windows squinting at the fitful sun, its walls pink or whitewashed according to Mother's whim, its balcony painted a shiny liver brown (as Mother called it) like the windows and doors. This was the haven I remember with its water and countryside, and its smell of salt and vegetation. Despite the Boat House being my first home, a permanent place, it was a place of constant movement – Laugharne where nothing ever stayed the same.

As I began to play with the children in the village, I discovered how tiny I was for my age with soft curly hair, upturned nose, hazel eyes, 'Too much acid in your system!' said Mother. She called my stomach 'delicate' and my limbs 'dainty'. 'You're a Thomas', she said, of my

Caitlin, Dolly, Aeron (aged 7) and Shelagh on the Boat House veranda.
(Photo courtesy of Rollie McKenna).

physique and my digestive upsets. When I was tactless she applauded and said I was like her – direct – not devious and Welsh. She approved of my temper, when I screamed and taunted my brothers in frustration: 'That's your Irish side.' I can't say I ever felt like a Macnamara but maybe she was right. My temperament was Welsh, I argued with her in later years, just like Granny Thomas; I was garrulous and sociable, interested in others, partial to gossip but not unkind, and wounded by criticism. Tactlessness and impulsive speech must come from my Irish side, or so I told my mother, who was famous for her unguarded remarks and a generosity I always hoped to share.

I remember a photograph of me in black-and-white, a thin girl with straggly curls. The dress I was wearing was red with a small floral print. The unknown photographer brought back in my mind the bright colours Mother always wore and sometimes chose for me. She was fond of a canary-yellow quilt skirt, which made a circle when she pirouetted. On walks she would cartwheel, her skirt like a glorious waist ruff. My red dress was cut plain and straight and I left the dashing to my mother. Ignoring the homely advice, 'blue and green should never be seen', she mixed yellow and turquoise, red and gold, 'though perhaps not for you'. Rupert Shephard, the painter who became my aunt Nicolette's second husband, told me how my mother and her best friend, Vivien John, went to the Café Royal in home-made costumes inspired by Botticelli's *Graces*. Laugharne was a small stage but my mother kept her style. One woman remembered her striding down the main street in the late forties wearing a black velvet skirt with a white blouse: 'Not at all what we were used to . . . very striking though . . .'

A Walk Around Laugharne

My mother and I often went on walks starting along the cliffwalk, the trees a dark arch overhead with light flickering in long, thin tongues through the branches. Through the trees you could see the sands below whipped into narrow ridges and imagine water serpents wandering across them. The foxgloves and ferns grew down the cliff and I longed to run down headlong to the shore but couldn't with my mother, who was always striding ahead. Loping along, with our dog Mably biting at our heels, I could just keep up with her, an Olympic walker who only just avoided being classed as a runner. Full of life, we ignored piles of stone overgrown with ivy and green lichen – the houses of long-dead people. Emerging from the untidy trees we climbed over stiles and barbed wire fences, laying jackets over the barbs, to fields of a green never seen since. In my memory, the fields are full of celandines, primroses and a few rogue daffodils. Gorse grew on the slopes.

As we neared the farm of Delacorse, ducks and fowl wandered free across the sloping farmyard. But as we approached Mably, to tie a piece of string on his leather collar, he would jump up. 'That bloody dog,' Mother said without passion. She never called him by his name; sometimes he was 'disgusting' or 'vile'. He was a dog who never kept still – a half collie that would herd us as soon as we moved. I loved him and his brown, white and black patches and collie face; he looked the way a dog should look and I was surprised when children with dogs of other breeds claimed theirs as a 'proper dog'.

One day Mother decided that after the farm we would head towards the highest spot in Laugharne, Sir John's Hill. The air was heady with honeysuckle, all the way. From the top of Sir John's Hill, we could see the sweep of shore with the Strand and the Grist, the castle, the cliff path and the Boat House below. 'We have to walk all the way back there,' I said, hinting that a fizzy drink and sweets might help if we took the village route. We usually had a pee behind the honeysuckle bushes before going back.

The cockle factory at the bottom of the hill, once a store for grain and malt, announced itself in fumes of vinegar, but Dolly's mother told us you forgot about it if you worked there. She lived within its heavy smell, a few houses along the Grist. Every spring Dolly said the sea levels were rising, and her mother would leave for the factory each morning afraid the house would be awash on her return.

We passed the cockle factory and walked briskly towards the Grist. We could see the high walls of the castle come towards us as we walked beside the Strand, a grey expanse of mud and sand flats, towards the humming pubs and shops. Ignoring the sweet shop, where she did not have credit, Mother headed for the Cross House Inn, a whitewashed building standing on its own, and made towards the back. 'Just saying a word to Crossmouse, see you in a minute.'

I waited outside, looking around the square for someone to play with. Mably sat down, turning his head from left to right. I looked towards the bus stop but only boring people waited there to go to Pendine. Crossmouse, the pub landlord, was more a ferret than a mouse with his sharp, small features and darting eyes, I thought. Seeing him and my mother locked in a goodbye embrace I felt a qualm of disgust, though I did not dislike him. He bribed me with bottles of lemonade and allowed me in the bar for short visits. After her call, Mother would report, 'Your father's in the Brown's, unsurprisingly.' I wondered how Crossmouse knew. News went round so fast in Laugharne I sometimes felt it was a danger to think.

Up the hill, we stopped at the sweet shop, where we owed £30. The shop was one of a list, including the butcher, general stores and off-licence, where we owed money. The shop lady greeted us:

'I threw a bucket of water over him, Mrs Thomas.'

She looked at Mably who had wandered into the shop after us.

'Always throw a bucket of water as I sees him, he's a terror.' added a customer.

My mother was all approval, but I ignored her and set to selecting the very best boiled sweets from the glass jars on the shelves and the counter. I liked the brown stripy ones, the colour of tigers: yellow, black, orange-brown and white. With Dad in mind, we chose yellow sherbets, the inside powdery and sickly sweet, and the shop lady pressed a huge gobstopper into my hand.

'I'll have some liquorice sticks too,' I said to the small, neat young woman serving me. She was the perfect 'egg in its cosy' Miss Price in *Under Milk Wood*.

'Say, "thank you",' admonished Mother, 'Say, "goodbye",' and, out of earshot, 'You have the manners of a pig.'

I was busy thinking whether I should have bought barley sugar instead of humbugs as we walked past the haberdasher, the butcher and the Davies' general store along the main street to the Infants School. The building of large rectangular stone had sash windows at giant's height so no one could look out. Next we passed the general store and I pressed my face against the shop window to see Alan Davies, a teenager with gangly legs, sitting on a full sack while his mother chatted with a customer, jumping to attention when she noticed him doing nothing. We poked our tongues out at each other then started on funny faces. I really liked him. We might get married when I caught up with him, my body thin and ungainly like his.

'Come on,' my mother said, as we climbed the steps to the Brown's Hotel. I could see my father's and grandfather's unmistakeable silhouettes sitting in the large bay window. Grandpa took off his trilby to

Dylan stands outside the Brown's Hotel with Ivy Williams.

scratch his bald head and, ashamed at my stare, rammed it on again. I'd never seen him without a hat, even at the dinner table. As we entered the bar, he and Father looked up from their folded newspaper where they had been studying *The Times* crossword, and soon my father started to play a game of shove half-penny and skittles with me. The other men at the bar seemed uneasy at our presence. The loud guffaws and horseplay – one man slapping the other on the back and everyone laughing in appreciation – stopped, until they forgot about Mother and me and the affectionate banter started again. 'Always the first one there, Bob. Never shy in coming forward is Bob.' I wondered what it was all about. None of my business.

As I held the wooden ball on the chain, set to fell all the skittles in the world – I had a good eye but no strength or tenacity – and let it go, my father and I followed the slow arc. The boisterous men were silent. One skittle remained. My father took over and demolished it.

'Mr Thomas,' called the lady behind the bar, 'what will it be?'

My grandfather was at the bar, uncertain what to order.

'A half would do,' said Dylan, looking at my mother. It was nearly lunchtime.

I could feel the relief in the bar when we left. Women were bad enough but children were worse. If we called before opening time we had to ring the bell and Ivy, or her husband Ebi, would answer the door as if expecting Scotland Yard, and say with relief 'Oh, it's you, Mrs Thomas . . . he's in the back.' The 'back' was Ivy's kitchen where she cooked lunch before the bar opened at eleven. It was there, my mother told me much later, where Father heard the morning gossip he transformed into *Under Milk Wood*. With a pint of warm bitter in his hand, my father would sit at the comforting table while Ivy put casseroles in the oven. A plump, middle-sized lady with a half-pint to keep Father company, she was queen of the gossips, relating the latest scandals while serving the customers. In the evening she and Ebi would play cards with my parents in the bay window; there are photographs to prove it, as someone says in 'The Outing'.

Once Mum and I had collected Dad, we set out along King Street. My mother had to slow down as usual to walk with my father, me trailing at the rear, when Mably, whom we had forgotten, suddenly appeared around a corner of Victoria Street. A dog with spindly legs, one of his lady friends, was at the bakery door and he shot towards her. When my parents turned around they found me watching transfixed by the doggy coupling. Mother's foot could not part the two dogs who had a cheering audience of children, so she urged me on.

We heard the water from a bucket hitting the dogs as we rounded the corner. My father looked on impassively, pretending it wasn't our dog.

It was a five-minute walk home. On the way, we passed the cottage where mother bought Staffordshire plates from the travelling salesman who came to Laugharne once a month. I stopped to look at the scrap of garden on the sea edge where daisies and wild flowers grew, and saw Mably slinking down the slope to the shore, going the long way to avoid us. 'Come on,' urged my parents who had reached the shed, half-way along the cliffwalk.

As I caught up, my father said that he was busy today and not to make a noise, then disappeared into his shed.

'What about Dad's lunch?' I asked, knowing the routine.

'Ivy gave him something,' said my mother. Meanwhile he stuck his head out to say, 'Cat, will *you* tell her to be quiet today?'

I was indignant at his distrust, which was brought about because I sometimes encouraged my friends and Llewelyn to press their bicycle bells, sing and bark with Mably as we passed outside the shed. If it was a lucky day, Father would push his battered kitchen chair back from his kitchen table and open the door to shout at us, waving a weak finger. His response was all I wanted and we would go hollering away down the hill and on our way to bike round Laugharne.

One day, I was free-wheeling on my bike down the slope by the shed, with Mably biting my front wheel in a frenzy. He managed to block my descent, and I flew over the handlebars. As a result, my father was dragged from his work in a black mood, and called my mother, who took over and sent him back to write. I still have the gravel scar on my left knee.

'What a blubber baby,' Dolly said unsympathetically as Dr Hughes from St Clears dressed my wound. It was worth the discomfort and fear of permanent damage for a scene of high drama, myself the centre of attention.

Dylan seated at his desk. (Photo courtesy of Rollie McKenna).

I always knew whether my father was working or reading his forbidden detective novels. If you passed and heard nothing he was reading, for as soon as he picked up his fountain-pen he spoke every word out loud. For him, the sound of the words was integral to the poem. Sometimes his voice was loud and booming, at other times I had to put my ear to the thin door to hear his mumbles. It seemed like a secretive, incantatory rite.

In the mornings my mother would tidy up the shed, rearranging pictures of writers torn from magazines. One was of Walt Whitman, one of W.H. Auden, looking like any academic with a shaggy tweed coat, dark shirt and tie, and there was a thickly bearded D.H. Lawrence.

There were also celestial characters in washed-out blue by William Blake, along with the more earthly figure of Blake himself, and there were reproductions of Modigliani, Chagall and Picasso. When the pictures started to curl round the tin tacks pressed into the wooden shed walls, Mother threw them away.

She would also remove the most sodden books from the low, free-standing bookshelf or the cardboard boxes that served for storage. All books in the shed or the house got damp, and flecked with what looked like salt. Drying them out made the pages as brittle and break-able as cream crackers. Mother would gather and flatten out the screwed up pieces of paper on the floor, rejects from work in progress. Finally, she would make sure there was enough Tizer – the brightest of orange fizzy drinks, guaranteed to dye your insides – Dad's favour-ite. I was sometimes allowed to finish up the dregs when she put a clean glass on the table.

To keep him warm while he wrote was an anthracite stove which in retrospect seems very dangerous in a room with so much paper floating about. He always had a smouldering Woodbine in his mouth, its ash not falling until the last moment, and a saucer of stubs. Helping my mother clear the mess, never destroying a discarded paper, I would look through the window in front of the desk where Father could see the estuary, across the Tâf to the hills where our ancestors lived. The whitewashed Pentowin Farm on the Llangain headland had been home to his uncle and aunt, Jim and Annie Jones. They did not make a success of farming and moved to try their luck again. The other window in his shed looked over the estuary to Sir John's Hill, the subject of his first poem when he moved to the Boat House.

After a morning at the Brown's, and a fry-up of cockles, dabs from the estuary or eggs from the dairy, Father would walk to his shed. It was two minutes from the house but away from children most of the time. He had to stay there from two till seven as my mother would lock his door (as her contribution to his literary output) and he seemed to accept this. At seven, she would be dressed up and ready for the evening at the Brown's, leaving us to fend for ourselves. I was left every night, at six years old, to look after Colm, and we shared the bedroom at the top of the house, separated from our parents by a narrow landing. I lorded it over the front bedroom window while he was tucked into a corner.

On numerous occasions I was woken up by the sound of drunken song, as revellers from the Brown's Hotel or the Cross House Inn reeled down the path to the door. From my window above the front door, I could see the garden terraces and the boozy group winding their way from the cliffwalk gate. As she always did, Mother rushed in to rustle among the clothes hung behind Colm's cot, to grab a skirt to dance in. I could hear the gramophone and raucous laughter but Colm slept through it all. At night, I was in charge and felt protective.

I could never keep up with Mother's need for physical exercise, though I shared her wish to get into the sea at every opportunity. The citizens of Laugharne were not so tolerant of the new family when they discovered Mother and sometimes me swimming at low tide with nothing on.

'They must've been hiding behind trees,' complained my mother. 'I never saw anyone.'

After these reports, I modestly kept on my voluminous navy-blue knickers in the water and out. Even Mother remembered to wear a bathing suit, though more often she brought extra knickers and bra for herself and extra pants for me. Tongues continued to wag. When not swimming, we went boating, Mother handling the oars like a sailor which, in the town, triggered comments of disapproval and admiration in equal measure.

Visitors

Caitlin with Aunt Nicolette and Aeron in the garden of the Boat House.
(Photo courtesy of Prosper Devas and Lady Monson).

We told our visitors that sailors were shipwrecked along the ill-fated Cefn Sidan Sands; those washed up at Ferryside from the 1886 Teviotdale wreck were buried in the St Ishmael Churchyard, within view of the sea. My father would always give them his version of the wreck. He was eleven in October 1925 when the *Paul of Hamburg* foundered between Llanstephan and Ferryside, and its crew and canary were carried ashore. He could see the remains of the four-masted white schooner wedged in the sand from the train on his way to Ferryside and Johnstown with his father. This was the side we could hardly see from Laugharne, the other side of the Llanybri headland where the Towy and the Gwendraeth meet the Tâf. For years afterwards, fragments from the wreck were washed up on the shoreline. My cousins thought he was telling an adventure story from the comics they all devoured but I told them it was real.

Mother and I heeded Booda's warnings about when and where to swim. As I was the only one other than Mother to enjoy splashing about in cold water we were often just the two of us. But I could not abide sunbathing which Mother indulged in even more than swimming if there was even a hint of good weather. Mother used to sun herself in the back garden on a large towel, basting her skin with olive oil. Visitors couldn't believe it when they walked round the veranda and saw the semi-naked woman. One of them, a young Swedish student studying Dylan's work for his thesis, was once discovered surreptitiously viewing her. He was renting a room in Laugharne and everyone agreed he looked like a blond Greek god. During the day, he was meant to be interviewing my father but was barred from him in the afternoons when Dad disappeared to write.

Dolly's niece Shelagh and I often gave our teddy-bears tea parties behind the garden shed. We served berries from a bush that grew over the outside lavatory, lovingly arranged on little pieces of broken crockery found in the mud. Booda had told us with much writhing how the berries were poisonous. One day we decided to invite the Swedish student to tea. He seemed reluctant to accept the invitation until we brought out the deciding phrase, 'My father would like it.' So he relinquished his viewing spot behind the sitting-room window on the second floor and joined us on the sharp rocks behind the shed.

We served the berries and diluted Tizer from the second-best cups Granny gave to Mother, which I had sneaked past Dolly's vigilant eye, and we made tea-time conversation, asking how long he was going to stay and when he would be going back to his Swedish university. He told us about his thesis on my father's poetry of place, and said this was a great opportunity for him. He was so affable we nearly forgot we were waiting for him to clutch his stomach and die. 'I think you've eaten enough,' I said, snatching the plate away. (We had only pretended to eat.) Nothing happened during the day, but we never saw him again. He had a bad digestive upset and when he recovered it was time to go home. I felt a sense of satisfaction, the glow of a job well done.

I wondered whether my mother would have behaved like me in a similar situation where action was required. Perhaps I did take after her. Whenever I felt that no one was listening to me as I babbled on, I slammed doors or screamed with frustration. Mother would proudly say, 'You can tell she's her mother's daughter.' When I acted off stage as if I were on, she said, 'Always the centre of attention . . . I know where you get that from.' Llewelyn commented, 'Exhibitionist!'

In addition to the Swedish student there was a constant stream of people passing through. One visitor was a university professor, an old man of forty or so. One day we were on our own in a dinghy and he moved to touch me and before he laid his hand on my shoulder I knew his intent. Pretend nothing, pretend ignorance, I thought to myself. He might stop. Coldly and wisely I looked at him as if from a vast distance, measuring the look in his eye, the slant of his shoulder, the curve of his spine as he tilted his way towards me, unsure of his footing. The rubber dinghy lurched to one side and he fell on the side of the boat near me. I looked away to the hills opposite. He edged his bottom closer. The dinghy began to sag at one end as he extended an arm to encircle my waist. 'Take the paddle,' I said, 'We're about to hit the rocks.' It was nearly worth drowning to see his incredulous face. 'The tide's turning, can't you see?' I added, infinitely older. He lunged at me, sprawling; the paddle floated away, the dinghy spun around on its axis, hit the rocks and his arm dropped. All the while I was watching him with disdain. At six, I knew what he was about.

I can see him now, a large man drenched and frightened by the current that swept us on to the mudflats and rocks, while on shore Mably barked with excitement. Later, I told the professor about the legend of the whirlpool near the Boat House, adding my own legends of boats foundering on sandbanks and drowned mariners all witnessed by my father. He blanched and said he thought the current unusually strong. I could manage him. He gave me my first gold ring, which I wore at the christening. I took it because it was so splendid and it fitted me. I wasn't going to tell my parents, so I accepted the ring as compensation.

Other summer visitors included Angharad Rees, a girl younger than me but with the same interests, sharing the obsessiveness required for creating crockery houses on the rocks. She would arrive every year to stay with her family at Cliff Cottage, a stone's throw from Dad's writing shed. She had long, light brown hair which she wore round her shoulders like a pashmina, with no awareness of her blossoming beauty. We immediately liked each other, squelching about the mud for a piece of china or glass, optimistic that this one, yes this one, would be covered with a multi-coloured pattern.

We would disappear so long that her parents would send scouts to the Boat House to tell Angharad supper was ready. We would often be eating Dolly's welsh-cakes, fresh off the bakestone (or plate of the Aga), vying for a seat round the kitchen table, sharing one as we giggled and dropped crumbs.

One day, sitting in Cliff Cottage, being quizzed by Angharad's parents and other grown ups, I told them about my schoolmasters (one was called a rude name – something like 'Bum') and all about my small world in Laugharne. 'We kept asking you questions because you had such a charming Welsh accent! You made us all laugh . . . but we tried to keep serious faces,' they explained. Dr Linford Rees, Angharad's father, was a professor of psychiatry.

Visitors to the Boat House included John Davenport, Norman Cameron and the painters Henry Treece, Fred Janes and Mervyn Levy, who provided constant intellectual stimulation while we were in Laugharne. My father's best literary friend, Vernon Watkins, would visit with his wife Gwen, while Augustus John stayed at Castle House and painted Dylan several times. He joked with malice that Dylan and Caitlin lived on air, passing the time reading Shakespeare in bed. My parents had also previously stayed at Castle House, which was the cold but furnished home of the hospitable Richard Hughes and his wife Frances. Keidrych Rhys, editor of the magazine *Wales*, his wife Lynette and eventually their two sons lived across the estuary at Llanstephan. Dylan was best man at their Llanstephan Church wedding where Lynette held a bouquet of fresh wild flowers.

Keidrych Rhys and my father had known each other since 1938

when my father started working on *Portrait of the Artist as a Young Dog*, and Keidrych remembered Dylan still found time to read thrillers and the Russians, including Chekhov. My father visited Keidrych at Llangadoc and Llanybri, near where his great uncle, Gwilym Marles, the Welsh poet, preacher, social reformer and teacher, lived his vivid life. After 1934, the Swansea writer Glyn Jones paid several visits to Laugharne and he told me about a visit they made together to North Wales to visit Caradoc Evans, who greatly influenced my father's writing. There were also visits to Laugharne by journalists like Mimi Josephson, who described my father's 'old tweed jacket, open necked shirt, grey flannels and pair of plimsolls'.

Transatlantic visitors included John Malcolm Brinnin, who organized my father's reading tours in the United States, and Rollie McKenna from Massachusetts, who photographed us all. Professors, students, writers and photographers from Wales, England, Italy and the United States were all made welcome.

But I preferred visits from my mother's family from Blashford in the New Forest and Chelsea. Aunts Brigit and Nicolette would bring cousins for me to play with, and Granny Yvonne Macnamara, Mother's mother, grand and remote, would come too, acknowledging children but communicating chiefly with the adults.

One day as Aunt Nicolette, Mother and I sat on coats and rugs by the harbour while the cousins climbed the rocks and looked at the estuary, Nicolette told me about my birth in London during the war, my mother embellishing the story as we ate crusty bread smeared with olive oil and garlic, messy and delicious.

On 3 March 1943, in St Mary Abbot's Hospital, Kensington, my mother suffered her usual painful delivery. My mother claimed that her uninhibited screams went unheard because of the deafening noise of an air-raid. She said she was consoled to know the world was falling apart as well as her own body, but complained with fury that Dylan was conspicuously absent.

After a week, Nicolette, who was living in Markham Square and helping her sister whenever she could, was sent to find him. She looked in all the usual Chelsea haunts: the Eight Bells, the Six Bells (if it wasn't already bombed), the Markham Arms, the Cross Keys and the King's Head, and eventually found him at the Anglesea Arms in Fulham Road, in the middle of an amusing story. She stayed on the edge of the crowd, someone offered her a drink, and she joined in the laughter, till 'time' was called and she remembered her mission – to take my father to Caitlin and his new daughter. 'He was such a good story teller and so funny. He made you forget everything.'

Mother added that he eventually turned up unwashed and unshaven, in an old dressing gown and slippers, while she hid in the bathroom. She was not sure whether she screamed at him or refrained because the other mothers were looking as he stood at the bottom of her bed, looking out of place, and forgetting to ask after the baby.

In the Manresa Road studio flat in Chelsea she was greeted by chaos. Newspapers, bottles and empty cigarette packets littered the floor and every surface including my cot: a basket cradle prepared lovingly by Mother with clean bedding. The woman next door with the eighteen cats peered in to see if she could help. The smell of cats was strong. Mother said she was not going to stay. After the initial shock, Caitlin settled down to clean the ramshackle studio, the stove behind the curtain, the antique bath and shared lavatory. Clean towels and blankets were 'borrowed' from Nicolette and my nappies were washed and hung out in what remained of a building opposite after a recent air-raid. After all this, she felt better, forgave Dylan the taxi she had to order to come home when he failed to collect us from hospital, and took delight in her baby.

'Your father was very cunning,' she told me. 'He knew he'd gone too far, not collecting me from hospital, leaving the flat in such a mess, so he brought Theodora and Constantine [Fitzgibbon] after the pub back to the bomb-site the first evening.'

Mother did not like to make a scene in front of such companionable and generous friends, who even lent Father a room in their tiny flat for him to work, but Nicolette chimed in with disapproval. This is where I was brought up, apparently, for the first few months of my life, regularly left alone at 7 p.m. sharp, leaving me to the cold, the falling plaster, the rain from the glass roof, and the bombs, while Caitlin and Dylan – as Nicolette said with mounting disbelief – went off to the pub.

Mother returned one evening, she said, the air-raid siren wailing, to find the bombs falling and the filthy cat woman with me in her arms. Indignant that the smelly woman should be holding her 'beautiful, feminine, small-boned, delicate baby', she ungratefully snatched me back. Forty years later, she blamed the drink, saying it never occurred to her to stay at home rather than follow the nightly routine, 'I would have lost Dylan if I had.' During their marriage, Dylan never once stayed at home in the evening, always preferring the pub. Mother told me that Llewelyn, between three and eight, was left with her mother and sister at the family home at Blashford so that she could be with Dylan in Chelsea, Soho and Fitzrovia. 'Why keep me?' I wondered but did not wish to ask. I suppose an immobile baby was less trouble to look after than an older child.

I left Nicolette and my mother to chat and got up to mischief with my cousins. When they all left for Tenby, where they borrowed a holiday home every year, I knew there was trouble. Llewelyn complained I had handed out the bikes to my cousins including his and it was damaged. They were not used to free-wheeling, I explained, but Mother was furious and used the brush she used on my curls on my bottom.

I told Granny at the Pelican, where I often visited to escape Caitlin's unpredictable temper. She couldn't help sympathizing with my mother this time but when she saw my red behind she was more sympathetic to me. Yes, I could stay the night if my parents agreed. Grandpa had disappeared into his study, a slight figure, hat and pipe attached.

The Pelican

B efore Grandpa settled in Laugharne, I remember him as a reserved silent man but not the sullen, scowling figure of later years. Before Laugharne, after he retired from teaching, he had no real escape route or bolthole, staying with relatives in a tiny cottage at Llangain or with us at Southleigh. The Pelican, where they lived on the ground floor, was a substantial Georgian house with multiple rooms and outhouses as well as a basement for storage. The largest room, facing the street, was designated as Grandpa's study and out of bounds for everyone else. He was surrounded by his books and far from Granny's beloved prattling friends and visiting relatives.

Granny came from the working class area of Swansea but her roots

Granny Flo and Grandpa D.J.

were rural, from the Llangain farmhouses. Her sister still lived there with their brother who was considered 'slow' and incapable of looking after himself. The educational divide between Granny Florence and Grandpa David John Thomas was evident; Granny knew her place as mother and homekeeper, though she always had a maid to help when they lived in 5 Cwmdonkin Drive, not far from the grammar school where her husband was head of English.

In the Pelican I often slept with Granny when things became unbearable at the Boat House, slipping into the hollow of the mattress and pulling the thick eiderdown up to my ears to keep warm. The eiderdown was half a foot deep, filled with duck down and covered in pale hamster-coloured cotton. The sheets were made of a furry material and the pillows plentifully stacked on a bolster, all designed for the cold Welsh bedrooms, which were never heated in those days.

Granny taught me how to draw sheep, using a wavy outline to suggest the woolly pelt. I would spend hours drawing them sitting at Granny's table in the kitchen/dining-room. I wanted to know how she cooked the rice puddings that she was either putting into the oven or taking out to show me the browned surface of the milk. Sometimes, she would feed me the top and put the rice back to form another skin.

If Granny's sisters and cousins were visiting, I was ignored while they talked to each other in Welsh, getting in each other's way as they prepared tea. I was shooed off the table and my drawing-pad of sheep put on a smaller table for me to continue.

Granny would object. 'Daddy doesn't like Aeron to speak Welsh.'

'Well then, Aeron bach, it's the English is it we have to speak to you,' said Auntie Dosie indulgently.

They were talking about funerals when they changed to English.

'Is that enough?' said Aunt Polly in a worried voice, when Granny said she paid 6d into her funeral book once a week.

'Well, I've got the hams ready,' explained Granny.

I wondered why hams were needed to bury her. I trailed after them down to the basement where large hams like off-colour bagpipes hung on hooks from the ceiling gloom. The sight of these ancient things made them erupt into Welsh again. I was not noticed in the dark and, creeping back up the stairs, I left them to it.

'Oh, there you are,' said Granny on her return. 'Good as gold. No bother . . .'

Mother saw me differently. When I behaved badly, my mother would swell with family pride, and say, 'She's spirited that's all. Can't think where she gets that from!' and give me a painful cuff, warning me that was enough.

Another aunt put her arm around me, 'Looking after our Florrie, is it . . .' She brought me a box of Terry Gold from Swansea which I would have emptied so quickly as to make myself sick, so Granny hid it.

'Well then, we'd best be laying the table,' said Granny, queen in her home. I was forgotten once more as they all slipped into Welsh again and brought out the white embroidered cloth, the welsh-cakes, fruit cake, Victoria jam sponges and sandwiches to the table, with the thinnest of crockery and silver cutlery. All my aunties seemed to have false teeth, taking them out for discussion when the men were not around, complaining about the fit and the expense. I picked up one of the cups, off-white with twisting leaves of elegant brown and black, and looked at it against the light of the window.

'You'll be putting that back, Aeron bach?' said one of the aunts. It was the Welsh way of saying, 'Put that back now, it's a precious porcelain cup . . .'

My father was first in for tea and was offered the second best chair – the best upright Queen Anne was always Grandpa's. He pecked Granny on the cheek and then the aunties. The sisters were flying around like a flock of starlings, alighting on the table then rising, wings flapping, on their return flight to the stove where the water boiled. My father was asking after relatives and family friends and being given the awful details of births, illnesses, marriage and death as Grandpa entered, his hat and glasses obscuring his thin, pinched face. He was greeted with plumped-up cushions and a rug which he rejected. Several deaths were reported by the women, who had come to rest on the hard dining-room seats.

'He had a good life,' said one, 'like his mother he knew when to go.' They all nodded.

Then, 'Poor Jack still in the infirmary and his children dead before him . . .'

'It'll be me and Bob (poor boy) that'll have to look after him like we did Mr Evans when he came home to an empty house . . .' reported Aunt Polly. 'His wife Mary died while he was under the knife, having his stones removed . . . terrible shock . . .'

Grandpa's expression grew blacker, and Dylan, who had been listening with great intentness, suddenly said, distracted, 'Where's Cat?'

I piped up, though I should not have been following the conversation so closely, 'She's coming, she told me, because she says I have to go home with her after tea.' I was not pleased about that: Granny and I had plenty more to do. She was going to let me make a rice pudding under her directions, listen to a story I was writing and let me put in seeds for my own flower patch in the garden.

The front door bell rang; everyone looked up and I jumped up to let Mother in. She was wearing tulip colours: a yellow blouse with tulip red spots. Her red skirt rustled as she moved. I wondered why she wore party clothes so often. Pausing outside the tearoom, she dabbed scent behind her ears and flounced in to incredulous stares, followed by hasty, polite greetings. I saw Aunt Polly taking furtive glances at her but whether from admiration or disapproval I could not tell. 'Hello, Cat,' said my father in relief. Suddenly he seemed too big for the stuffy room.

A large pot of tea, another mat and a strainer were carried in. Tea was poured and the beautiful cups and saucers were handed out –

even one for me, with admonitions. When I forgot the warnings amongst the flurry of plates, cakes and local gossip and placed my tea on my drawing of sheep, a vigilant aunt took it away. I ate slice after slice of Victoria sponge.

My mother complained that the teas were far too tempting. The aunties did not look overweight to me on their diet of welsh-cakes, but diminutive and brown like the tea they drank from morning till night.

Granny's behind wavered in the air. She was bending to pick up a piece of fluff or a crumb she had seen on the carpet. She often interrupted our little activities to pounce on an offending speck, pulling herself up painfully with the aid of her stick.

'Get up, Florrie,' barked Grandpa, heard for the first time, looking like a tetchy and abstracted professor with his glasses, pinched face and trilby. It struck me that Granny was very frail when I saw her struggling to regain her balance, but most of the time I did not give her weakness a thought.

After the tea I managed to persuade Mother to leave me with Granny because the next day was Sunday and there was no school, which I had been attending for a week or two. A clean set of clothes was delivered in case I became dirty. The next day Granny and two lady friends from Carmarthen took us by car to one of the congregational chapels on the road to Pendine. Outside the chapel there were only two other cars and we felt grand alighting from ours. The rest of the congregation arrived by foot and bus, chattering in Welsh, unlike most of the residents of Laugharne.

The chapel worship swelled until the climax of a long sermon in Welsh in which the preacher made concessions now and then by translating, 'And you'll burn, burn, burn.' Before giving more away, he returned to Welsh. Granny told me he was talking about Hell. 'But we're all going to Heaven,' she told me. 'Hell is just for the bad people. We wouldn't want to be with them, anyway.'

'Daddy doesn't believe in God,' she explained to me on our return to the Pelican. 'He's an agnostic.' It sounded quite grand. Grandpa flashed us a bitter look as he passed the little group of women in the kitchen to go to the outside privy, without acknowledging me again.

He wasn't always that way, I thought, thinking back to when we used to visit them at their temporary home, Blaencwm, in Llangain. They lived in the smaller of two cottages with Florence's sister and brother, Great Aunt Polly and Great Uncle Bob. My grandfather hated the move and had nothing in common with the relatives in the next cottage. My father called it 'this house too full of Thomases'. Whenever my family ran out of places to live with rent to pay, they fell back on their parents, sometimes for months on end. My mother said D.J. (as my grandfather was known) was maddened by my grandmother's constant visits next door to her sister 'yakking away in Welsh' while Bob, who was 'twp', said very little. Even my grandmother noticed how morose her husband became, retired and away from his few congenial friends in Swansea.

D.J.

He seemed pleased to see his son when we stayed with them at Blaencwm for several months in 1947. They could discuss early versions of Dylan's poems including the now famous first drafts of

'Fern Hill', based on his memories of childhood holidays spent in the farm nearby. My father obviously felt at home in this part of rural Wales and produced other poems and prose including 'Memories of Christmas', which was expanded into 'A Child's Christmas in Wales', which relived his Swansea childhood. 'Fern Hill' was written in a tiny upstairs room.

Grandpa didn't seem to mind me, then aged four, trailing after him as he gardened at Blaencwm. He showed me the brook that ran down the side of the garden in a little gully which you couldn't see straight away as ferns grew down the side of the slope. He forgot to warn me about the dangers but I knew about them, as I was constantly warned about keeping away from the open cesspit at the bottom of the garden which looked like a muddy pool. (When the cesspits were to be emptied, Grandpa disappeared on a visit to Swansea. He felt this was an indignity too far for a fastidious man and it reminded him how far he had descended in the world.)

I remember once when he let me walk along the edge of the lawn where it was cut into a springy wedge, perilously holding on to his fingers, until we reached the greenhouse. It was a jungle of tomato plants filling every inch of the glass frame. Grandpa had to bend his head and I stood beneath a wooden shelf. Then the miracle occurred. He picked one of the red fruit from the overhanging, thickly inter-woven green stems and offered it to me. The smell of freshly gathered tomato was so pungent I would not bring it to my nose but held it like the globe of the world to take back to Granny. 'Now that's a tomato,' he said before I could make the presentation.

Uncongenial surroundings and lack of friends made him think fondly of his teaching years spent predominately in the Swansea

Grammar School of the twenties and thirties, a short walk from his home in Cwmdonkin Drive. In particular he missed his colleague and close friend W.S. Davies, the head of Classics, whom he used to meet every evening at the bar in the Uplands Hotel. He was known universally as D.J., not David John or Mr Thomas.

He was known by the students as 'Soldat' for his military bearing and the way he entered a schoolroom, his gown wrapped around him. He was also known as 'Snipe' because of his fondness for the word 'guttersnipe' which he used to describe anyone slacking. He was an exacting man who demanded full attention in his literature lessons. The boys would innocently ask him to recite Malvolio's speeches from *Twelfth Night* and he would grasp the hooked stick used to raise and lower the sash windows and stride declaiming across the classroom floor. The boys loved these exhibitions and left the stick propped in a prominent position by D.J.'s desk. His love of Shakespeare and the classics, and his passionate recitations, made life-long devotees of literature of future bank managers and accountants.

Daniel Jones, a fellow student of the grammar school (later a composer and my father's best friend), told a story proving that D.J., though strict, was less so with his wayward son – who went on to fulfil his own early ambition to be a poet. Dylan and Daniel were 'mitching' from school one afternoon and D.J. stopped them with the admonition, 'Be careful the headmaster [Mr Trevor Owen] doesn't catch you' and let them go.

First Days at School

On Sunday evening, Mother collected me from the Pelican after my weekend stay but when I went to school on Monday the chapel hymns still rung in my ears. She told me I'd soon learn to read and write. I preferred being read to, I said.

On my first day of primary school my mother must have been there, but I can only remember dawdling along the walk to the village, inspecting the daisies by the gate that lead up the cliff-side, looking over the bay on the other side and wondering why I always craved company when I was so happy alone.

Teacher Gwennie, an assistant acting as class head, wore glasses and a voluminous twin set. As photographs prove, she was young and plump but looked to us the epitome of kindly authority. Neither Granny nor Mother possessed a large bosom so it exercised an inordinate fascination. Miss G., replete with pale blue or pink botany-wool-covered chest, conducted us like an orchestra, a chalk her baton. We stood up and sat to her command, chanted her words in repetition, picked up our pencils and laid them down as she indicated, all choice taken away about where we should be and what we should be doing. I never heard her raise her voice.

From the beginning, I was entranced by the thrill of the 'Janet and John' reading books with their perfect Spot dog and a mother I could not recognize. So this was what it should be like; Miss G. was going to reveal all I was missing. Getting ready for a friend's fifth birthday party, after a game with Spot in which no one was dirtied by hysterical paws, the fictional little girl Janet had her long, straight hair parted

Teacher Gwennie.

and beribboned. A sadist mother pulling your hair out at the roots, shouting at you, was not part of Janet's world. Janet and John never quarrelled to disappoint the perfect mother, I thought, thinking of Llewelyn and our vicious encounters. My presents for parties never looked like the carefully wrapped boxes they carried, not that my mother didn't struggle to tuck in the loose ends. I can remember a doll falling out of the wrapping before it could be handed over.

When Miss G. started teaching us the words under the illustrations I was pleased that some could be read by their sounds alone, phonetically. I knew there were some nasty ones that my father had pointed to in the nursery rhymes he read to me, though I was getting too old for them, but I had high hopes that Miss G. would browbeat the words into order. I was anxious that we would finish the Janet and

John book too quickly. We were learning to read so fast. I was relieved when we finished one and I found there was another in the series, Book II.

Miss G. wrote the words on the board in large, joined writing so we could chant the words. Contrary to current-day practices she introduced us first to every letter in the alphabet which we had to recognize, chant its name (however remote from its sound in subsequent words) and then write it. One way or another we all learnt fast, having little difficulty in pronouncing 'A' as 'ay' or 'ah' or any other surprise. Capitals were taught from the beginning.

At break time, we were given milk and allowed to run about in the playground without supervision. We were in a prisoners' courtyard with high brick walls and asphalt floor, flanked by the two buildings: the youngest children's class and the hall in one, the primary school proper in the other. Miss G. sometimes coached slower children during our breaks while we skipped, played hopscotch or stood on each others' backs to try and scale the walls. By the end of term we could all read simple words and sentences. Now that someone had showed me the key I tried the phonetic method on new books: Enid Blyton's *Noddy* and the *Old Woman Who Lived in a Shoe*. When it didn't work I tried guessing from sense or by the alternative sounds each letter seemed to possess.

When my father took me on his lap to read *Grimm's Fairy Tales*, comfortably settled into a capacious armchair, its back to the sitting room window with a view of the estuary over the balcony, I concealed my new knowledge in the fear he would stop reading aloud to me. It seemed to suit us both, and he tactfully never enquired how my reading was going as I tried not to follow the words on the page.

The first job at school was to take off your winter coat and welling-ton boots if it was raining. The cloakroom smelt of wet animals drying when all our coats were hung neatly on the line of hooks. I sat next to one of the boys, as the boys were separated from one another because they would pinch each other or slip marbles into each other's collars to drop down the back and fall noisily on the floor. The moment Miss G. wrote something on the board, her back to us, the boy next to me would wrest the pencils from me. 'Tommy Davies,' she said, 'give Aeron her pencil back.' With supernatural powers, she kept order.

Fighting

In my first term at school there was a lively diversion enjoyed by the children of my class. At first Mother walked me to school but Dolly soon took over, with Mably following. He wasn't invited or encouraged but followed Dolly at a respectful distance. Dolly some-times shouted at him but remembered to feed him with leftovers of chips and welsh-cakes. But, like Mother, she preferred humans to animals. One day an incident occurred which made Dolly laugh so much when recounting it to cronies she had to cross her legs to avoid peeing herself.

Richard Lewis, the milkman, lived in Newbridge Road, opposite the primary school, with his yapping corgi. The dog usually sat on the windowsill. I saw the milkman sometimes at the Boat House, carrying the tin cans of milk. They were not unlike steel billy cans but with a stiff handle. Sometimes, Dolly would intercept Dicky the

Milk (as he was known) on his rounds and bring the can herself, pouring its contents into a jug kept in the cold larder behind the kitchen. This particular day, I came out of the school and could see the corgi through the window opposite, baring its teeth, his jaw opening and closing as if he were gasping for air, and to all intents and purposes having a heart attack.

'What's the matter with him?' I asked.

Dicky loomed up behind the dog.

'Not him,' I persevered, 'the dog.'

'Oh, he's always like that when he sees Mably,' said Dolly.

I looked around and saw Mably sidling along the wall to the window.

By now, the corgi was in the terminal throes of a fit, throwing his body here and there, foam dripping from his mouth. Mably joined the din, each dog barking from different sides of the closed window, challenging the other. We looked at the spectacle. Even our teacher had stopped to watch the two dogs, the smaller one on the other side of the window making more noise than Mably.

'What's the matter with them?' she asked.

'My dog can't abide the Thomas dog,' explained Mr Lewis.

Then Dolly alighted on a surprising and daring idea. 'Let the buggers fight,' she said, 'Might get it out of their system.'

I was horrified, not liking the image of Mably bloodied and limping.

'What, open the door?' asked Mr Lewis, looking interested.

Before I could list objections, the milkman's door was open, the corgi was out in the gladiators' street, and the dogs bit into each other, crying and barking, whenever their mouths were not sunk into each other's flesh. 'That's enough,' I screamed and tried to pull Mably away from the scrum. I was nearly bitten for my pains and started yelping myself. At that, Mr Lewis scooped up the corgi, a writhing mass of fury and frustration, and threw him unceremoniously through the door, ramming it shut. Mably seemed surprised to be free, made a couple of cursory barks towards the wounded Corgi back on his windowsill perch, and then turned to follow Dolly and me to the Boat House. There was a tuft of hair missing from one side of his flank and one eyelid seemed swollen and bleeding but otherwise it had been more sound and fury than real damage.

We applied Dettol to Mably's wounds. Usually when he returned with a scratched nose or other minor wounds we treated him without knowing the circumstances.

'Can I put the Dettol on this time?' I asked. 'Look what he's done to Mably,' I said to Dolly, referring to the assailant, forgetting the corgi was still a grown puppy.

Dolly's solution to the corgi's fixation with Mably seemed to work. Richard Lewis said the corgi would now jump off the windowsill when he saw Mably and retreat into the yard in the back with the chickens. The corgi went on to live a long, uneventful life according to Mr Lewis.

When we moved up to the main building with the older children the first change was our introduction to Scripture class. I was delighted to notice that we had regressed to story listening and could while away our time hearing about the wild characters of the Old Testament, like Joseph's wicked brothers and kings or pharaohs who would not listen to God and suffered locusts and boils. Stranger things had happened in the fairy stories I knew where beans turned into sky-scraping trees and carpets flew with young Aladdin or witches on their back.

When we arrived at the Psalms in the systematic reading through from Genesis onwards, and read about cool waters and hidden, secret valleys, I felt a different quality of landscape from the Grimms' land of sombre forest. The fantastical golden geese and frog princes made way for the people and places of the Bible. I imagined myself walking through the valley of Psalms at my death. During Scripture class, I rested my mind in this place of shadows and mystery. It was my favourite lesson.

Entranced one day with Jonah and his dark world inside the whale, I was suddenly caught up in a scuffle with two girls. When the teacher came over to investigate, they turned on me saying, 'It was her, Miss.' My mouth dropped open with the enormity of the lie and, with my mouth still slack from the shock, I was led to the headmaster for five sharp cane strikes upon the hands. Hands bright red and smarting, I stood outside my class with my head hung low, reluctant to go back in.

'What are you doing, Aeron? It's in or out, isn't it, not blocking the doorway.' It was Miss G.

'Oh, Miss G . . .' I burst into tears and nestled in her arms as if I were a baby of five again, my head comfy on her bosom.

'Has he been at it again?' she asked, though looking at my red hands she didn't need an answer. 'So long as it's the boys . . .' she said, then thought better of saying any more. 'Now come along,' she said kindly, 'we'll face them together.'

She opened the door and gently pushed me forward. There was a respectful silence. Miss G. and my regular teacher left the room after

a whispered exchange. Unusually, there was total silence until I understood that all were observing an unwritten ritual, mourning my
temporary loss of dignity. Boys were caned harder than girls.

Miss G. took the opportunity to ask how my reading was progress-
ing. I told her that my dad still read to me but I could now follow
many of the words.

In fact, he was not the first person to introduce me to reading. In
1946–7, when we stayed for a year at Holywell Ford in Oxford with
Margaret and Alan Taylor, they read to me daily along with their two
daughters, Amelia and Sofia, both younger than me.

Reading with Alan (often referred to by his initials A.J.P.), a television personality, academic historian and don at Magdalen College,
was a highbrow session. My father read us childish things but Alan
stretched our minds into new worlds. We squeezed into Alan's study
in Oxford or later St Mark's Crescent, London, as he puffed on his
pipe and read *David Copperfield*, regardless of our capacity to fully
understand. He had a deep, authoritative reading voice and sometimes
I would lose the narrative and just listen to the rhythm and pace of
Dickens' prose. I liked both Margaret's and Alan's reading sessions
but felt more comfortable with her because she petted us and called
us 'Duckey'. She kept telling us what a lovely time we were having,
which we knew already, but we forgave her. Her reading from *The
Secret Garden* was a daily treat. In her private sitting room, she played
the piano and encouraged us to sing. Margaret was my father's patron,
much to Alan's disgust.

At that time my father read to us only sporadically, either in his
Romany caravan parked in the grounds where he worked for the
BBC or even more squashed in the Taylor's summerhouse. He read

nursery rhymes, some of which we knew and recited with him, and told us about the characters who lived along the river bank in *The Wind in the Willows*. Living on the banks of the Cherwell River, we could easily relate to animals there.

It was in Oxford that I had one of my numerous near-death experiences. In London as a baby I had been left in a glass studio under the bombs; a little later there was the shooting incident at Majoda when I was hidden in the hearth away from the bullets. Still to come was the time I dodged a car twice within thirty seconds in South Leigh. I was nearly killed as I crossed from one side of the road to the next, my mother unable to intervene. I belong to a breed known as 'ditherers': to go or not to go, to walk this way or that, are heavy burdens of choice for us.

During the summer months in Oxford we went boating on the river where willows dangled in the shallows. I was sitting on the rim of the boat, looking at the green water, dipping my fingers to grasp some floating green stuff, when I fell in. The water rushed past my face and I realized this was what they called drowning. I plummeted down, green tendrils overhead. The urgency to breathe was overwhelming. Then the surprise occurred; Mother in a huge movement came to join me, pulling me up by the collar. Surfacing, we found arms outstretched to pull us back into the boat.

'That's the last time you come on the boat,' said Mother, hitting me soundly. Even my father looked concerned.

Later that day I found him walking by the Cherwell instead of working and tagged along not speaking. He stopped by the stretch of river where I'd had my boat accident and said, 'You're not going swimming again, are you?' He saw my discomfort and quickly added, 'Just joking, silly. I expect you wanted to swim with the fishes.' We stood looking at the green flashing shapes under the surface.

'I thought Mum was a fish,' I said. He looked puzzled.

'When she dived for you?'

'Yes,' I said positively, 'a stripy silver one.'

'I'd have been one of the water animals from *Wind in the Willows*.' I looked puzzled in my turn. 'Maybe a sleek otter,' he said doubtfully, 'or more like a water rat like Ratty,' he elaborated, with a shiver. 'That's what I'd be.'

He promised to read to me the book where they came from . . . sometime. I told him what Margaret was reading to us and even A.J.P. and he looked approvingly.

'I can't understand everything when Amelia's father reads to us,' I admitted, 'but I listen and listen and think about the story even when I go to bed . . . But I can understand *The Secret Garden* all right. There's a garden with a little girl who plants flowers and things and there's a poor cripple boy too. When Sofia cried, Margaret said he gets better in the end, so she stopped.'

Dad was looking distracted and I knew he had to go. I always gabbled as fast as I could to get in the most possible words before he thought of something he had to do more pressing than talking to me.

'Tell me more later,' he said in a parting shot.

By the time we arrived in Laugharne, we had settled into a reading routine.

After his weekly bathing session, he came out steamy and wet as an African warthog, passing me Dolly Mixture from a perspiring hand. Mother arranged the tiny sweets along the rim of the bath as part of the preparations. 'There's probably more in the bath,' he advised and I dived into the wet room, the walls weeping with condensation, grabbing sodden sweets, then rushing out again to see Dad drying off and open to entreaties.

'Will you read to me.'

'Where's the book?' he asked and I knew that my chances were good. 'Where is it?'

I rushed off to the bookshelf for the Brothers Grimm, and handed it to him. We settled down to enter the dark world with relish.

'If you could choose, who would you like to be best in 'Red Riding Hood'? asked Dad.

'I don't know, the woodchopper with the axe.' He seemed to want a better answer. 'He comes along at just the right time.'

And Dad suggested, 'And maybe Red Riding Hood herself as she wins in the end.' Maybe, yes, I thought, imagining myself with a dashing red cloak.

We concentrated on new stories from Grimms'. Soon enough he was as absorbed as I as maidens fled in terror of wolves and other brutes. While he read, I photographed him in my mind so as not to forget.

Once I chose Struwwelpeter just as Mother arrived brandishing nail scissors; we were delighted. He continued to read as Mother cut his nails (not his fingers or toes) and tied his laces, often left undone.

I took the scissors, 'I'll cut off your hands now, shall I?'

'No, only my little finger, please,' he said, in a matter of fact way, as if ordering a small white loaf from the baker.

My mother lost her temper and snatched the scissors back, cuffing us both.

The reading sessions with Dad were only once a week, unfortunately, but school was every day and I was gaining more friends there as well as a Welsh accent to sound like everyone else. Even the teachers spoke with a lilt.

Kissing Clive

Clive was one of the boys caned for stealing at my primary school. He stopped me one day on the cliffwalk and kissed me on the lips. I did not tell Dolly about the incident but she soon learned from Booda that we had repeated the experiment more than once. The cycle shed, which was nearer the house than my father's shed, had no window over the estuary so even the birds could not see us. Booda reported seeing us come out of the shed, bending down to show Dolly how he looked through the loose boards to see us 'doing things', as Dolly reported. After that, I saw Clive every day at school but tended to ignore him. Booda reported everything of interest to Dolly in his deaf and dumb language, making more noise as he grew excited, never leaving the kitchen chair by the larder, a cup of tea by his side. He mimed Clive jumping up from our clinch in the shed, shouting, 'That man is spying on us!' and pointing at the eye between the planks. He showed us surprised and disconcerted though he couldn't hear our words of recrimination. He then showed Dolly how the bikes fell on top of me in my embarrassment.

Dolly tackled me and I told her, 'I'm not doing that any more. Clive and I go round Laugharne on our bikes.'

'Well, don't lend him Llewelyn's bike.' Dolly sucked her breath in with the imagined consequences, 'You'll cop it if you do.'

'Well, we'll put it back good as new before Llewelyn's back,' I said, remembering with a sinking feeling. The fender had already been bent due to a free-wheeling accident outside Dad's shed the day before.

'He'll be back before you look round,' warned Dolly. He was due home from school in a few days, she reminded me. 'And don't let that Clive mess with you neither.'

The world for Dolly was made up of men waiting in the dark for unsuspecting women, particularly those who worked at the Boat House. In her mind, men hung from telegraph poles, loitered in the alleys behind the outhouses and hid under the redcurrant bushes by my father's shed. I always wished Dolly well when she left the house during the dark afternoon hours in the winter, hoping she would come back safe and sound.

But Dolly knew how to look after herself, she said. When the Polish soldiers were posted near Laugharne during the war, she told me, she never went out with them, up Sir John's Hill, without her hanky. I wondered why she always had a cold. Perhaps the Polish soldiers gave her colds. 'Oh yes,' she said, 'Never did it without taking my hanky. I wasn't born yesterday.'

I was half-way through my second year at school before the school inspector arrived, a grey man with grey tufts either side of his mouth and a white stripe of hair falling over his forehead, like a badger. I was introduced by the teacher as Dylan Thomas' daughter.

'Good morning,' he said gravely.

'I'm Aeron Thomas,' I corrected calmly. 'Dylan Thomas' daughter' is not a name, I thought, in a fury of indignation.

Later that day I heard my name called yet again, but it was only the nurse to check for nits, which she did regularly. Afterwards I went over to Granny's, close to the school, with a large bottle of white stuff to put on my hair and leave overnight. Granny complained about the girls who had obviously given me nits as she bound an old towel round my head and sent Grandpa to leave a message at the Brown's that I'd be staying the night.

'No more sleeping six to a bed,' admonished Granny, knowing my weekend habit of staying with any family that would have me. Next morning she shook my hair, lank and viscous, and combed it with a tiny lice comb over the sink. Her own hair glowed in a halo round a pretty face. 'I'll have to boil your pillowcase,' she said.

Clive had an older brother who told him that kissing was not enough, so he asked me if I knew what we had to do in order to brag that we had sex. His brother was insistent and I understood the pressure. Finally, he persuaded me 'to go' with a gang of older boys who seemed to know about the subject. I was seven years old and curious to know what all the fuss was about. The brother, a heavyweight boxer in build, unlike Clive, was offered first 'go'. He told me to lie on the rock face immediately below my father's shed.

The rock was known locally as 'spots' because of the effect of lichen sprinkled all over it. His friends formed a circle round us, leaving a gap so that the children looking through the cliff railings could have a good view. Clive's brother hovered over me, then held himself above me in a press up position.

'Go on . . . pull them down,' he said, tugging unsuccessfully at my baggy navy-blue lisle knickers. I looked up at Clive who was peering from the railings with the others. The rock under me was digging into the small of my back.

I didn't think much of this sex business. You had to take your knickers off, lie on a jagged rock and have a big boy suspended over you, and an audience.

'I've got to join my friends now,' I said, indicating the crowd, and with a shrug he let me go.

'You have to keep your knickers on so that the boy can't see your navel,' I informed boys and girls who asked for information. I wasn't sure how dangerous it was to kiss but it was a bit boring, I warned them. Obviously, the big boys were bored because they were diving off the 'spots' in their underpants. Later, I told anyone who asked, 'If you kiss too long you get a baby.' My reputation as a seven-year-old sex expert was growing.

I failed to understand why the possession of a famous father left my school friends cowed but not impressed while this sexual expertise earned me respect and awe. When Mother took me shopping to Mrs Davies' general store, called Manchester House, Alan looked at me strangely from behind the counter, then came over to help my mother with her purchases. He went to pick up a box of Persil soap suds, gave them to me with a wink and a 'I know what you've been up to' look and said, 'That's what your mother always buys.' 'Thank you, Alan,' said Mother. 'I nearly forgot that Dolly wanted some . . .' she said adding the box to Virginia tobacco sachets in her rigid cane basket she held in the bend of her arm.

'I'll tell your mother,' shouted one of the older boys as they ran up the path alongside the shed but my indifference infuriated him. If challenged I would resort to the truth that nothing happened. Mother was excellent at divining the truth: 'Long practice with your lying father and all those lying Welshmen.' For her, the Irish were never afraid to tell the truth, regardless of consequences. For Granny, to doctor the truth meant not hurting people and avoiding conflict. I belonged to the Welsh school.

The Boat House Rats

Aeron and cousin Prosper.

One day when we were waiting for the rat-man, Dolly said: 'Go and see what Colm's crying about.'

I was happy to do so as this might mean I'd see the great rat killer coming down the path before anyone else. Colm was lying in his pram outside the front door. The kitchen where Dolly and everyone – except my father – lived was next to the back door. I ran up the narrow stairs to see Colm. He lay with his mouth open, crying loudly. As soon as he saw me he gave a beatific smile. He really liked me which made me love him but jealousy was a dark living presence. As soon as I accepted Colm, my mother made a point of holding him adoringly, excluding everyone, especially me, from the ecstatic moment. Hugs and lingering pats on the head for me had dwindled noticeably since Colm had been brought back from Carmarthen hospital in a tightly held, shawl bundle. Fortunately Dolly, though charmed by him, seemed to enjoy my company more.

One day before I could put into action a little plan of revenge, a loud cry was heard from the outdoor lavatory. I pelted down the stairs again to see my father rushing into the kitchen, holding up his trousers with one hand, and jumping on to a kitchen chair. His arm in a sling, braces falling down over his two-sizes-too-big trousers, he kept shouting, 'Rats.'

Colm's yells from his pram by the front door could be heard faintly, drowned by Dylan's screams.

'Stop screaming like a stuck pig,' said my mother, very calm.

'Millions of them,' said my father, perched precariously, his heavy short body listing to one side.

'Get down from there! You'll break the chair,' ordered Mother as she screamed at Dolly to find a broom.

'With whiskers,' said my dad and added, to me because no one else was listening, 'with a tail a foot long.'

'Yes,' said Dolly, 'I was just sweeping in the larder.' As she came out with a brush and various implements, she informed my father, 'There's one in the trap.'

This started him crying even louder, and he stepped on to the table. I could hear Colm's demanding cries, then my father shouting, 'Rats, rats, rats . . .'

'It was only a mouse in the trap,' I told him, as I went to join the fun outside. 'It's all right. It's dead.'

My mother rushed past swinging the broom, 'Move! Find some stones.'

I reached the back garden with a jump from the balcony, ignoring the steps, and yanked at unyielding boulders, pulling some loose stones from the wall. I could hear the broom being hit against the corrugated roof of the lavatory. One of its walls was the cliff, which dripped water and mildew and was alive with beetles and spiders. I'd sit there for hours, transfixed, betting on whether the cockroach would move right or left or fall off. Dad would read the newspaper there. Granny said that Grandpa had a bit of a library in their lavatory but would never leave his Bible there because of the damp.

'I can't see anything,' Mother shouted.

Father started screaming again.

Then I saw it: a dark-grey-mud-coloured creature searching frantically for a place to escape. It was difficult to tell where he was in the mud. I kept still and he boldly ran the full length of the wall under the downstairs veranda and disappeared under the big shed. 'Mother, I found one,' I announced.

'That bloody dog,' she said, turning to swipe Mably but hitting Dolly instead. The dog got hold of the broom, thinking it was a game, and my mother fell in to the mud. She turned her full fury on Dolly, asking why she'd got in the way instead of helping, and Dolly rushed up the steps away from her. From the veranda she watched us, laughing so much she had to hold one leg over the other to stop herself peeing. Mother and I, the brave ones, were left to deal with the rats.

'You can tell whose daughter you are,' she said to me afterwards when I helped clear up the cockles that had spilled out of a bucket where they were soaking.

Once we scaled the steps from garden to the kitchen, we found Dolly helping Dylan off the table: 'There won't be any more rats, now. Mrs Dylan has chased them under the shed.'

Interviewed about her days in the Boat House, Dolly later told a journalist, 'Mrs Dylan threw me down the stairs once . . . yes, she did, honest. Oh she had a temper that one . . .' she said admiringly. 'Bloody good hiding she used to give me regular. And language, well, I wouldn't like to repeat.' She also told me later about her own mother, 'My mother used to say, "What, that Mrs Dylan been having a go at you again?" And I'd say, "No." Wouldn't have wanted to see them have a go at each other.' Dolly's mother was so tiny and brittle that my mother would have blown her over with a couple of words. I could see her toppling, brown and vinegary, ready for the pickling jar. But I didn't say anything.

Once the crisis had passed we remembered Colm, who was sobbing quietly. He must be getting very tired, I thought, as I scooped up the cockles. I crept up the stairs to see him tear-stained and blinking with fatigue. I wrapped him tight to make him feel secure, and put him under a bush in the garden. Out of sight and out of mind, I said to myself with satisfaction – another cliché not allowed at the

Boat House. He fell asleep at once. I stood meditatively looking down at him, sucking two fingers, a secret habit not discarded for decades.

'Aeron,' I heard an urgent, secretive call. It was Clive looking over the cliffwalk wall.

'Up in a minute,' I answered in a loud whisper. No, I couldn't go cycling, Dolly was taking me shopping. Maybe later.

When he heard the name of Dolly, he made a grimace, 'My mam says she's got an awful tongue on her.'

I glared at him. It was true Dolly had been regaling the kitchen gang and half of Laugharne with the weaknesses – alcohol and fights – of his parents. She also said that Clive was 'neglected' – never a clean shirt there. I didn't know how to defend Dolly and I knew she shouldn't have said such things about someone who was part of our gang.

'You can't say she doesn't know how to cook an apple and black-berry tart, fair play though,' I said in mitigation.

After our shopping Dolly and I made our way to the Grist. Dolly's house was an apologetic, low-slung cottage made from uneven stone blocks, the whitewash peeled away by weather and sea water. Inside, a tidemark ran the length of the small hall and below it the paper had turned the colour of dry seaweed. Dolly opened the parlour where the furniture was covered in sheets looking like shrouded sarcophagi.

She picked up the sides of a sheet to reveal an upholstered chair in ancient brown damask stained by seawater. 'See what it's done. Ruined everything.' She revealed relics belonging to the three-piece suite including a pouffe made from brown leather. I crouched to feel the stiff, unyielding leather and nodded my head in sympathy. 'My father used to rest his feet on that,' she said, replacing the covering. 'And the worst was I wasn't here when the tide came into the house to help Mam take the best stuff upstairs. I was visiting my sister. My mother was ever so quick, running to the neighbours up the road, using their phone to call my uncles and brother.'

I imagined Dolly's mother, a diminutive figure so thin you might think someone was starving her, running like one of the Boat House rats, a flash of grey in search of a bolt hole.

'But it was no good,' Dolly continued. 'By the time my brother arrived from work, everything was ruined.' She looked round, shaking her head, rocking back and forth in memory, squeezing her hands to her chest. I looked on in mute sympathy.

'My auntie's husband arrives too late on the Saturday two days later asking if he can help, the lazy bugger, and if there's anything needs disposing of . . . we know what his "disposing" means . . . selling it off to the rag and bone.' Dolly was not to be interrupted. 'The last time we used this sofa,' she said, pulling off its shroud in one dramatic flourish, 'it was for my auntie's funeral. Lucky she died before the water got it. You can seat four or five on it easy.'

I was beginning to cough and splutter with all the dust from the furniture.

'There,' she said, replacing the coverings, 'best not weep over what can't be undone.' I was trying to make out what this double negative meant when she became practical and everyday.

'Want some pop?' she asked conspiratorially. I loved pop and always drank a little of Dad's Tizer before Dolly did the top up tightly to keep in the fizz. We sat at Dolly's kitchen table and shared half a tumbler with a custard cream. 'My mam will know we've been here. You can't put anything across on her,' she said proudly.

The sea did, I thought, but then it flooded all the houses in the terrace. The hours at the cockle factory were long, and she wouldn't be home for hours to look for clues: shifted sheets or disappearing biscuits.

'Can I go and see the parlour again?' I asked.

Looking through the window I saw Clive hide behind the seafaring castle wall before reappearing, his head around the corner. I waved but he couldn't see that far. 'Can I go and play?' I asked Dolly who had joined me at the window watching Clive's head appearing round the corner like a sideways Jack-in-the-Box, then his entire body. He was crossing the square towards the house.

As he arrived at the door, Dolly opened it suddenly, making him jump.

'So that's why you brought your bike along,' said Dolly, 'not to help me with the shopping, is it?' Then relenting, 'I'll tell Mrs Dylan you'll be back for tea.' Dolly was kinder than she liked to pretend. I rushed for my bike propped against the garden wall.

'I knew you was inside 'cos of the bike,' said Clive. We went to his house, similar to Dolly's, to wait for our friends. We squeezed past the family bikes propped in the hallway. 'They make an awful mess,' said Clive, referring to the torn wallpaper. 'We could keep them out the back but my dad likes them ready like.' There was a strong smell of yesterday's cabbage and I was dying to go out and play. Clive started telling me about his family, how his father kept his money under the bed because he did not trust post offices and banks, and how he fell off his bike when 'on the pop'. He had been warned about being drunk and disorderly in charge of a bike when he collided with the local bobby. I knew 'pop' was lemonade or alcohol. Dolly told me that Clive's mother joined her husband in the pub. Dolly was severe with women drinkers; though to men who went to the pub every night she only said, 'Good riddance.' My mother, of course, was an exception.

Clive said he was going to leave school and go into the army as soon as he was old enough. He never had a penny to spend on sweets and drinks, though he managed to go to the cinema at Llanmiloe. I told him that he shouldn't leave Laugharne, but I was thinking of myself.

This talking, discussing and imagining was more interesting than kissing and all that. 'Got anything to show me?' I asked, all encouragement. He looked pleased.

'Yes, I've got . . .' He was thinking. He showed me the Swansea china, lustre teapots in a cabinet, medals 'won in the war' (liar, I thought), old razors and a war-time identity card. After rifling through a drawer full of cami-knickers and other intimate garments, he produced a powder compact, brooches, 'gold' trinkets and a frilly pair of 'best' lace gloves.

'You shouldn't be touching your mother's things,' I admonished.

If he'd been a girl it would have been different. I often tidied the lipsticks and tortoiseshell-backed hairbrushes and mirrors on Mother's pretty dressing table. He showed me his mother's hats and I couldn't resist trying them on, though they would have been a good nest for headlice which Granny said lived in clothes as well as hair. 'You can't be too careful,' I heard her voice saying as I tried a mohair beret which covered my eyes and nose. I pulled it off, annoyed at the bad fit.

At that moment the front door banged. 'That must be Eira and Gwyneth.' Clive then offered us all tea but when we stepped into the kitchen, with its lino holed and worn, and saw the unemptied tea pot, its cosy with a line of brown tea-stains round the hem, we lost our enthusiasm. I only drank fizzy drinks, cider or water, I said, in any case.

'Let's go and play Hunt the Cow,' said Eira.

As we were peddling slowly up the hill to Orchard Park – Gwyneth was the Cow and we'd seen her aim towards the council estate though we were meant to be counting with our eyes shut – I reassured Clive: 'Look, I'm having apple pie tonight made by Dolly. I won't forget this time.' His eyes looked hungry. 'I'll keep you a slice . . .' He wasn't satisfied. 'A big one.'

As we passed the house of Johnny, who was in his thirties, Eira said, 'He's looking at us from behind the nets.' But the nets were so grimy you couldn't see anyone lurking. Johnny opened the door, his huge belly before him, beckoning as we toiled up the steep hill.

'Don't go near him . . . he's nasty,' said Eira.

'Look, look, Gwyneth's bike's by there, down the side of the house!' shouted Clive, pointing to the house.

A moment later and Gwyneth's laughing red-framed face appeared from behind the dirty curtains. 'You never thought of looking for me here, did you?' she asked as we filed in sheepishly, our bikes slung on the scrap of green outside. Johnny went to find the sweets he kept in a jar and offered us tea which we declined. It was only one step away from having to climb on his lap, we agreed when discussing Johnny. Gwyneth was munching sweets so we knew we'd arrived just in time.

'Well, time to go. My mother's waiting for me,' said Gwyneth which was a lie as her mother was in Carmarthen at the market and wouldn't be home till five. We all trooped out while Johnny looked crestfallen and his old dog, sitting in his basket, beat his tail on the floor as we patted him before going.

I had to get home to supper. As I returned to the Boat House, I remembered Colm. Rushing to where I had left him, my heart jumped and I could feel my face prickle with sweat. No, not under the bush of yellow flowers, maybe further up the slope under other yellow flowers at the second lawn. We called the grassed ledges which Booda scythed 'lawns', remembering grander residences my mother had known. Colm wasn't on the second or even the third lawn and he certainly wasn't past the gate on the cliffwalk. My memory couldn't be that faulty. I pushed the gate open, my limbs shaking, when I saw my mother holding the baby Jesus.

'Colm! Is it Colm?' I cried.

'Who do you think it is?' said my mother, then casually, 'Someone left him under a bush, soaking wet.'

'It wasn't wet,' I said, admitting my guilt, my Welsh liar's quickness deserting me.

'No, I mean, he was wet – had a wet nappy full of shit,' said my mother.

I winced at her coarseness. Granny would have said 'a dirty nappy' or 'not a very nice nappy,' teaching the niceties of social behaviour and conversation. The important thing was that Mother wasn't cross, putting her arm around me, allowing Colm only the crutch of one elbow. I could never understand how some things sent her berserk, ranting and raving with flaying arms, while bad deeds, like trying to get rid of her golden boy, met with understanding. Llewelyn and I always called him the 'golden boy', accepting Mother's fondness for him as an act of nature.

'What's for supper?' I asked, taking advantage. 'Fried cockles for your father and me . . . egg and chips for you.' She knew I wouldn't want to eat the cockles we had picked yesterday. I would only eat cockles I was not acquainted with, from the factory in jars.

Dolly was preparing the tart I had promised Clive, rubbing half lard, half butter into white flour. A fine dust was settling on the kitchen table which she would soon clean, scrubbing away as if her life depended on it. I sat down with her niece, Shelagh, and her son, Desmond. She deftly sliced potatoes into fat wedges which would turn into chips. We sat round the table like birds in a nest, our mouths open, anticipating runny eggs with plenty of salt and lovely brown vinegar. Dolly grumbled as she cooked the eggs in olive oil which mother also used for suntan lotion and hair conditioner.

'Lard's good enough for the rest of us,' Dolly commented.

'Oh, give us a bit of proper fat,' we pleaded, encouraging rebellion.

'Is "She" out of the way, then?' Dolly asked.

Mother

You could often hear my mother banging around upstairs as Dolly finished her tasks quickly and efficiently in the kitchen, surrounded by her loyal subjects. Unlike Dolly, Mother's movements seemed unconnected to her: ineffective, graceless and uncoordinated.

Caitlin in front of the Boat House. (Photo courtesy of Tony Vilela).

Instead of the one movement to accomplish something, the sort of economy employed by Dolly, Mother seemed to need ten.

When Mother was preparing my father's bath, she would be up and down the stairs every minute. Like a whirlwind, she burst into the small, steamy kitchen, snatched the bottle of oil and shot up the stairs three at a time. She was like the heron in the bay, static and stately one moment then crashing into the watery world to devour a fish. One moment she would be sitting quietly on the grass, slowly rolling a cigarette, then she would erupt into our world to snatch or shout at me or brandish a hairbrush.

Yet things were different when she took the sun, stretched out on an old towel or ancient coat, cooking slowly or applying oil in wide, studied swathes on to her already perfect skin. Also, she was different when she danced and became a sylph. She trained as a professional dancer for a short time with the Isadora Duncan Company based in

Paris but when she danced in the chorus at the London Palladium she was sacked. The incident rankled over the years; she was as good as any of the other girls, knew how to keep time and could memorize a routine; she could do flips and cartwheels and walk-overs; she could bend over backwards, form an arch, holding her heels for support. She kept asking why they had sacked her, eventually realizing that she must have been drunk and forgot which leg to raise during the high kicks.

When Mother got married in 1933 she found herself in the role of mistress of mundane routines. I was always surprised by my mother's insistence on Dad doing certain things at certain times, especially as our freedom was often curtailed by admonitions to return for mealtimes and bedtime at hours determined by Mother.

My father was allowed to visit the Brown's Hotel for gossip and the crossword in the mornings as long as he returned at 1 p.m. for a lunch fry-up. Writing began at 2 p.m. – no excuses – in the shed. As I mentioned, Mother locked the door at times, particularly when he returned from trips abroad and was reluctant to follow his old schedule as laid down by her. On the other hand, he could count on her to accompany him to the pub every night from 7 p.m. till 10 p.m. Rowdy sessions back at the Boat House with pub friends tended to take place at the weekends when the workers could sleep-in the next day.

Within this framework of prescribed activities, my mother would collect my father from the shed for their pub session between six and seven, except for the weekly bathnight when he came back earlier and I was allowed to pester him for reading sessions.

Only my parents were allowed to use the proper bath put in

after Margaret Taylor's last visit. Running water was only installed after we arrived in 1949, and before that we managed with large rain butts, which we used to make our daredevil jumps from the veranda to the lavatory roof. Thanks to Margaret we were also one of the first families in the village to have electricity in our house. Before 1950, the town managed on paraffin lights. Mother was sometimes dismissive about our friend and patron, but I noticed all the bills were settled and decorating or domestic improvements made when Maggie came for a visit. When we first got the bath we could hear my parents overhead in the new bathroom while the rest of us still had to use the tin bath in front of the Aga, with water that soon turned cold and mud-coloured if you weren't the first. We could hear my father singing, then speaking in his low mumbled boom.

'He must be doing the parts from his play,' I commented.

'He'll be in there an hour or more,' said Dolly, 'using up all the hot water.'

I crept upstairs and listened outside the bathroom while the deep bass changed into a woman's sultry contralto. I think it must have been Dai Bread's wives from *Under Milk Wood*. Alternating between the bass Mrs Dai Bread One and Mrs Dai Bread Two, he continued.

He had explained the two wives to me before, on my insistence. 'Dai Bread – he's the baker – is married to two wives. In some countries men marry more than two wives and that becomes a harem.'

'I hope you're not going to marry someone else, too,' I said, 'unless it's someone we know like Alice's mother. She'd be all right.' But the thought still worried me until Mother said that it would happen over her dead body. I knew then it couldn't happen because Mum was in charge.

Mother said Ivy Williams from the Brown's had told him about a man with two wives which had started him off: 'In that case, probably you couldn't have told the difference as men always go for the same type,' she commented.

'But Dad said one of the wives was a gypsy and the other wasn't in the play he's writing.'

But Mother lost interest. She didn't discuss his work with me, but I gleaned all I could by careful listening. They must think I'm deaf and stupid, I thought, as I heard my father become the Rev. Eli Jenkins:

> By Cader Idris, tempest torn,
> Or Moel yr Wyddfa's glory,
> Carnedd Llewelyn beauty born,
> Plinlimmon old in story,
> By mountains where King Arthur dreams . . .

The Rev. Eli Jenkins and the others lived their lives in our house. After a hard afternoon creating dialogue, my father would try out the lines with Mother as audience. As she struggled with a heavy black iron casserole pot to make space for Dolly's welsh-cakes, he would choose that very moment to read from the poet/preacher or Polly Garter or Mrs Dai Bread One, his voice skating from high to low pitch.

Without giving a sign that she heard, my mother would huff and strain to emphasize the physical effort of domestic chores. My father ignored these tactics and after a minute or two Mother would wheel round in a fury and say, 'Take that stuff upstairs.' Crestfallen, my father would gather his papers and retreat. The silence lingered behind him. Later, Mother would follow him and, for ten minutes or so, the voices could be heard again, my mother never interrupting.

After the bath and before they left for the Brown's, Mother rearranged Dad's spotty kerchief and dried his hair briskly in the kitchen to remove excess oil and water. He was rolling his tongue around the word 'Struwwelpeter', and I answered with 'Rumplestilskin'. Approvingly, we both rolled our gobstopper words while mother continued to tidy up Dad for his pub outing. When I later read that my father looked like an 'unmade bed' in America I knew it was because Mother was missing. She looked after him and even darned his socks and sweaters, albeit in different shades to the garment; bright pink or orange elbow darns on a speckly, tortoiseshell ribbed sweater or green wool on grey socks: 'otherwise no one would know all the hard work I put into it, a grey darn on a grey sock would be invisible!'

Treading Fish

Anything Mother did in the way of housework was an enormous effort and took a long time, whether it was cooking a huge Irish stew or seeing that we were all turned out tidy and presentable. She much preferred to be outside the house and often went treading for fish.

Treading was a well-known pastime in Laugharne when poverty forced the inhabitants to fish in this unusual way. Mother learned that at very low tide the only water left in the estuary formed gullies in the sand, away from the mud-lined shore. The flat fish would burrow into the sand, not attempting to swim in such low waters. So the trick was to walk along the gullies very slowly in bare feet. When you felt a movement under your feet, you had to bend and scoop the fish up and in one movement throw it and the accompanying wet sand on to the bank to be collected later.

A more dangerous extension to this way of catching fish was to use a long fork especially adapted for the purpose. I don't know what the original stabbers used to do but Mother waited for the movement under foot, removed her feet, then stabbed the fish. I was always terrified she was going to stab her own foot but didn't take into account how athletic and competent Mother was when outdoors.

One morning I promised to help. It was soon clear that the fish were not quick enough for my mother this time: she felt the movement under her feet, plunged her hands downwards and up in a scooping movement, and the poor fish came raining down on the bank. My job was to collect the stranded, gasping fish into a basket, a cane weave with a stiff handle which mother used for shopping or to carry her tobacco, Rizla cigarette papers and cotton hankies.

We set out when the water was at its lowest between morning and evening tide and the water ran thin tongues through the sand channels. Away from the rocks the mud turned into golden sand. My dress tucked into my lisle knickers, black plimsolls on my feet, I walked carefully to avoid pieces of china and glass rounded by the tide.

Mably followed us like a pig searching for truffles, rooting for crabs under the stones and in the seaweed that clung to where mud and shingle met. Occasionally, he slipped on the mud but could usually manoeuvre the rocks. His thoughts were perfectly formed but limited. He was no philosopher but knew what he wanted in the immediate future. He was like us children who optimistically left the future to look after itself.

On one treading expedition there was a drama, Mably yelping and careering towards us, disturbing the fish, the cardinal sin of the morning. 'Give me that basket,' said Mother as she swung her basket backwards to deal him a blow.

'But Mum, he has something on his nose. He's crying in pain.'

We removed the crab hanging on his muzzle; Mably looked deeply embarrassed and disappeared crestfallen towards the shore. I left the basket and slid deliciously into the water up to my waist. After a minute, I returned to gather the fish thrown on the bank. Poor fish. There would be no fish for dinner that day, I decided, and threw them back into the water.

Desmond suddenly appeared, bursting with news. He was a shy boy, difficult to tempt away from the safe kitchen area.

'What is it?' I asked.

Mother shouted from the bank, 'That's it. You're never coming with me again.'

I knew that was ridiculous – Mother never remembered her threats. But I'd have to keep some of the fish next time, poor things.

Desmond was panting with excitement. 'It's the rat-man.'

I looked back at Mother killing fish, with the basket left on the bank, as Desmond went white with apprehension even though Mother never shouted at him. She liked berating someone who might answer back.

'Ok. I'll tell her,' I said, and shouted the news to Mother. In a moment, she turned and was striding towards us, pulling down the folds of her skirt tucked into the waistband.

Running ahead with Desmond to see the rat-man, I skimmed over the familiar rocks and stopped at the back door.

'Mam says he's asking for Mrs Dylan,' he told me in a rush. That was a long sentence for him to speak, though he spoke endlessly to Booda in their version of deaf-and-dumb language.

Mother was coming back in a wet padded skirt like an American patchwork bedspread, an open-necked shirt, sleeves rolled above her elbows, carrying the basket with only three fish in it. She took a half-hearted swipe at Mably.

The man was standing by the kitchen door, staring in disbelief at Mother's beauty, and I stared him out. His eyes dropped. He was taller than the Laugharne men or my father and wore a funeral suit and a sad expression. One arm seemed longer than the other but then I realized he only had one arm. He had told Dolly he came from Aberdare and used to snare rabbits and shoot foxes but had drifted into chemicals.

'Lovely poisoners,' he said. 'I puts it by the holes careful like and all's I got to do is come back to collect the corpses. Simple really.' Dolly looked at him with awe. Usually she bowed to no one, saying, 'I'm as good as them any day.'

After talking to Mother, with me keeping an eye on him, he went into the pantry, expertly opened the mouse traps with one hand, prising apart the taut wires and pocketing a dead mouse 'to put in the sack'.

'No rats?' he asked Dolly, disappointed. 'I'll go and get my equipment.

No good filling the holes till I've tempted them with the bait and caught them, see.' And then he ladled out the DDT powder from a full sack.

'Don't put it where Mably can eat it!' I said. He looked at me as if I belonged to the rat family. Frightened, I slunk away to keep an eye on him from a distance.

He went outside and poked about between the bricks and behind the lavatory cistern, lacing the rat holes with more powder. He looked under the shed and along the wall where I had often seen rats run. 'They're partial to sewage,' he said and as everyone else had disappeared I took him to what might be sewage drains in front of the house, and pointed to the flagstones under the front door.

'There's a secret tunnel there,' I said.

After much difficulty he lowered himself down the steps facing the river opening, under the balcony, and entered the tunnel. I told him, 'It was smugglers put their brandy or whisky down there – when it was hightide they'd bring their boats in round the back.'

I then heard my mother say to Dolly, 'Has Mr Thomas come yet?' and suddenly remembered it was my job to call my father from the Brown's hotel to see the rat-man. In a bad mood, I jumped down to fetch him. What good would he be? He wouldn't show the rat-man the right places.

I rang the door bell of the pub and buxom Ivy answered. 'Your father's busy,' she said.

'I have a message,' I said, adding the magic words, 'from my mother.'

They were all frightened of Mother's temper and I was ushered into the kitchen at the back of the building. The room was full of a warm, smoky, meaty smell while the sash windows were steamed up and remained tightly closed. Father looked at me as if I were a stranger hopeful of a free dinner. He was sitting on a kitchen chair, his newspaper unopened, a pint of beer in a thick glass beside him. He wore a brownish Fair Isle jumper with brightly coloured woollen darns on the elbows and looked flushed. Ivy kept stoking the Aga and opening the oven door to tend a casserole and a rice pudding.

I delivered my message, noting the involuntary shudder the news provoked.

'Don't like rats myself,' commented Ivy.

My father said he'd be along soon, but I had my instructions and would not return without him.

'Sit by there in the corner, Aeron,' said Ivy giving me a lukewarm glass of lemonade. I made myself invisible and waited. I was in luck: Ivy continued her story, camouflaging the names.

'And She-that-has-seven-children no lies and as many fathers told me, honest to God, that the doctor refused her any help.' This was followed by a wink, head inclined towards my corner. 'Said she'd like to keep her womb, though, thought she might miss it.' Gales of laughter followed.

'And Danny Raye?' asked my father, who had chosen to forget me.

'Oh, him . . .' said Ivy. 'D.R.?' still trying to keep the subject anonymous. 'Singing,' she answered, 'if that's what you want to call it all night after drinking his pension away. Went to the Mariner's then the Cross House. Said he was King of Laugharne Castle and was going home to Castle House.'

She lowered her voice and allowed my father to take a sip of his beer while she took a draught of her own pint, giving us time to savour the story. 'There are some say there should be a petition but I won't be signing it. "Worse than courting cats," they say. "What a racket . . ." but it isn't every night, I say, only when he's got the money.'

I wanted to hear of punch-ups and swearing, to amuse Dolly. Ivy went on to say that there was a certain fat person they knew who ought to be stopped. 'There isn't a child in Laugharne that hasn't been asked to sit on his lap, girl or boy, he's not fussed.'

They had forgotten me and this time I knew who they were talking about. Last time I climbed on his lap he asked me to rub his legs to help the arthritis because nobody else would. I jumped off straight away. After that they returned to talk about people I didn't know.

I was falling asleep while Father remained awake and alert, hand on his beer glass as if it were the handle of a gun, ready to draw if required. He was laughing too. In my stupor I thought I heard the name of Clive's dad. I had overheard a teacher saying it was no wonder Clive stole things with a father like his and Dolly told me Clive's dad was sentenced at Carmarthen court to two years. Clive wouldn't talk about it except to say the police were 'criminals' to put him away. 'Those-of-us-in-Prison,' Ivy called Clive's dad.

'Do you remember the cup we won from Ammanford a couple of years back for darts that Those-of-us-in-Prison stole brazen like from off the bar here when no one was looking?' My father nodded. He looked as if he was being fed cream or tit-bits. I kept my head down to show I wasn't listening. 'Seems . . .' she dragged it out for effect, 'he's been bragging in prison that's not the only thing he's got that no one's found. Nice bits of Swansea china, pewter jugs and lustre wear off his brother's sideboard.' I stored away the information though I might keep it to myself. 'And him not even in prison for thieving,' Ivy finished.

'No, he mustn't have any more,' I stirred myself to speak as she went out to the bar to refill his glass. 'He's got a wooden arm,' I said. My father looked up at me, uncomprehending. 'The man who's come to poison the rats,' I explained.

'Oh,' he said, light dawning. He reluctantly pushed the chair away and stood up to go. 'Got to go Ivy. The rat-man cometh.'

'That's the rat catcher, Mr Morris,' said Ivy.

'They're not called that any more: "rat extinguisher", is it or "vermin exterminator" – something like that.'

'Llewelyn would have liked to be here. He could have shown him the best holes,' I said to my father as we walked home past the house with the monkey-puzzle tree.

'You can ask him if he's still there. Mum's not going to be pleased if he's gone.' Dad looked worried. 'I mean, 'cos you didn't come straight away to see him.' His expression darkened. 'I'll say I couldn't find you.'

'Or perhaps you met your friends on the way,' he said, perfecting my lie.

'I showed him the smugglers' tunnel but I didn't know how to get down it except by the rocks.'

'Yes,' Dad said, interested. 'They hid brandy in there brought over from France. Did the rat-man find any left there?'

'Oh, I don't know,' I answered seriously.

I stood by the fuchsia which grew at the entrance of our home in case the vermin extractor decided to pull up the flagstones. He was downstairs with my Dad but might be up any moment. Eventually, I found Mr Morris and my father drinking beer in the kitchen which was unusual as my father only inhabited the dining room. As a result Booda lurked by the shed outside cleaning cutting implements, unsure where he should be and waiting for his cup of tea in the kitchen after completing his tasks. Desmond was sitting on the wooden steps, impatiently. I decided that I belonged to all worlds and sat with the men and their beer hoping they might say something I was not meant to hear. Like a fellow sufferer, Mr Morris was inquiring about Dad's arm.

'Had a nasty fall? Ground's treacherous round here, all up and down.'

Dad said that there was no light down the Boat House path and he had fallen into a bush. He thought it had cushioned his fall.

'Better than falling over the side and on to the rocks,' I gave my opinion, forgetting to be a listener, not a contributor.

'Yes, yes,' agreed the one-armed man. 'You could have fallen . . .'

'. . . arse over tip,' finished Dad. I loved the expression, storing it for future use.

'Dr Hughes from St Clears came out for Dad last time . . . when he broke his arm.' I started, but caught myself at the mention of the word 'arm'.

At this second interruption, Dad looked less pleased so I refrained from telling them that Mother said the Thomases had chicken bones. She would take my tiny wrists and say I was a Thomas too, but so far all I had suffered were cut knees and hands.

Mother appeared suddenly, as was her custom, and both men jumped up in guilt.

'Well, Mrs Thomas,' he doffed his cloth Dai cap as if she were mistress of the manor. 'I'll be bringing a sack to tidy away the little corpses in 48 hours if that suits you.'

It could have been all the rat talk that gave Dad a bad stomach so for lunch Mother prepared him milk and sops with sugar and salt as Granny had always done. I was allowed to carry it to him as he lay in bed, a green Penguin thriller beside him, unread.

'Thanks,' he said like a dying duck in a thunderstorm (one of my new favourite forbidden sayings) as he propped himself up on pillows and I handed him a spoon.

Mother asked if I wanted to go to the village shops. I decided to stay when Dolly said that her niece Shelagh was going to come over with her mother, Dolly's sister Kathleen, and keep an eye on Dad.

'Da-a-d,' I said in a whining tone on my third trip from kitchen to bedroom and back with bowls and beakers.

'Ye-e-es,' he said, resigned to returning the favour with some banter despite not feeling his best.

'What would you say if we opened a cider for Kathleen and Shelagh?'

'It's up to your mother,' he said.

'Can't you say you drank it?' I suggested.

'Ok. Ok.' he agreed, anything for some peace. 'I'll say I drank it all if Cat notices. All right?'

I disappeared instantly, promising to check later, forgetting once we'd tasted the cider, we'd be braying like donkeys at the hint of a joke. It was warm and snug by the Aga and Dad couldn't possibly need anything more.

Booda, who had gone home with no teabreak, reappeared.

Desmond looked pleased, making movements with his head and hands to mime reading. With Booda, Desmond never said the words but gesticulated and acted out his meaning by pointing and bending, rarely translating his movements to us in speech, so that their conversation remained intimate. But Booda's accompaniment of noisy grunts, wheezes and whines was far from dumb. He and Desmond exchanged jokes and comments about cartoon characters. They laughed at Dennis the Menace and Desperate Dan, and emulated the bomber aeroplanes illustrated in the centrefolds of boys' comics, until Dolly told them to be quiet or Mrs Dylan would be down to see what all the racket was about. Often, Booda did not like us even to glance at 'Desmond's' comics, so we couldn't join in.

Shelagh was younger than me and I thought the difference was insurmountable. She had large, very bright blue eyes and black wavy hair framing a tiny, thin face. When the record player started, Shelagh and I watched Mother gyrate and jump on one leg. I told Shelagh the music was classical, not like the popular songs she was used to, such as 'Irene, Goodnight', and told her, 'She puts petticoats on and throws her arms about too.'

'Dolly tells my mam that she can do a backward flip and jumps about in the garden.'

'Leaps are called grand jetés in ballet,' I told her.

She wanted to know more. Like me she was inquisitive. I might forgive her for being so young.

Mably was drying off in the kitchen, his scent mingling with the smells of Booda's ancient leather jacket, Mother's stew and newsprint, rather like wet tar and vinegar. Booda produced a pile of comics. These were passed between Booda and Desmond, both enjoying

Dennis the Menace's latest prank. Desmond would never dare do anything naughty but he could dream.

They continued their noisy exchange. Booda's laugh was low and chesty and Dolly put her finger to her lips when he laughed so loud that he started coughing. He showed us a picture of Dennis up a tree evading irate neighbours while Gnasher nipped everyone's ankles. He pointed to Mably, who looked up and Booda extended his leg to rub his shoe on his ribcage. Mably grunted appreciatively.

'Don't you get too comfy now,' Dolly warned us. 'He'll be here soon and sorting you out.'

We remembered Llewelyn and the anticipation both chilled and warmed us. It all depended on his mood. He was due back from his grand school, Magdalen College School, and I wondered how he would like the new recruit, Shelagh. Desmond would have trouble with his allegiances, lending Llewelyn Booda's comics on the sly.

Christmas Holidays

Llewelyn broke up from school a week or two before Christmas. He arrived while we were sitting around, grumpy and ready to establish who was boss. He had to occupy the second-best kitchen chair by the door as Booda had the one by the pantry, the best place because it was furthest away from the door and Mother's dramatic entrances. It was as if he'd never left. Llewelyn ate a large slice of tart and was soon in a good mood, agreeing we could play Hunt the Cow on bikes, and yes, I thought, his bike was back in the shed, returned by Clive at the last moment.

My father was keen that Llewelyn should become a pupil at a fee-paying school. Both parents thought that it was a great opportunity, a first step to academic achievement. For Mother, Llewelyn going to Oxford was natural, as her own father went to Magdalen College. Boys were always given the first choice for a formal education with the Macnamaras and brother John was sent away to school while his sisters relied on erratic governesses. My parents' friendship with A.J.P. Taylor, as well as other academics and students, must have had some influence.

Llewelyn had to leave for Magdalen College School after just one year at the Witney primary school and the experience distressed him for the rest of his life. Llewelyn disliked his new school and found it embarrassing the fees were left unpaid so often. On one occasion, he was sent away but unhappily returned when a benefactor stepped in. In a last-ditch attempt to make his contempt of school clear he decided to do badly at his exams. Assiduously, he answered all the questions wrongly and received abysmal marks. He waited for his mother to open the report and realize that he was not public-school material, making all his efforts at failure worthwhile. According to him, she threw the report in the bin without looking at it.

Llewelyn disliked the rules and regimentation of the public school. He also complained that his parents did not once visit him in Oxford. While my father was keen that his son should achieve academically where he had failed (leaving Swansea Grammar School with no pass in school certificate except for English), visiting his son was not considered essential. When Llewelyn came to choose a university, he opted for Harvard in Massachusetts, as far away from Oxford as possible. By that time he had good enough results at school to choose any university and at Harvard he was immediately upgraded to the second year of studies.

It soon began to rain so, rather than play Hunt the Cow, we decided we were going to play Blind Man's Buff, organized by Llewelyn, the master of revels. The more the merrier, we decided, and Dolly was pulled into the dining room with screams and protests. Booda stood as onlooker, instructed to keep his eye on the stairs for intruders. I grabbed Shelagh, and pretended to spank her, so Booda understood it was Mother who might appear at any moment. The rules of the game were explained and we started. A tea towel was knotted around Desmond's head and he looked uncomfortable and frightened as it fell over his nose. He was turned on his shaky axis and promptly fell against the dining-room table.

'Oh, push it out the way,' said Shelagh.

'Mrs Dylan will kill us,' said Dolly, thrillingly.

'Move around,' commanded Llewelyn.

'Ow!' wailed Desmond.

'Go on,' whispered Dolly.

Shelagh was ducking and swerving like a fly-weight boxer, followed by Desmond and pushed by Dolly from the rear. Mably sat on his haunches under the table biding his time. Llewelyn told us we were cheating, shouting from the sidelines, so we all crowded into Desmond, allowing ourselves to be caught.

As I was having the blindfold tied around my eyes, I caught a glance of Booda clapping with excitement. Then someone pinched me, someone else pulled my hair and I felt an extended foot before I fell over someone. 'Caught you,' I cried. 'Your turn.'

Shelagh pointed to Booda who was laughing so much the tears

were gathering in the leathery furrows of his nose. 'He can do it, I'll keep watch,' she offered.

Soon Booda was 'blind man', with Shelagh installed at the door. He was moving very slowly and deliberately, extending his arms in a circular motion. We avoided contact, bumping into each other. Unexpectedly, Booda accelerated and caught two of us, one in each hand. He made a loud sound of triumph, beaming with his full fish net, as we squirmed in his vice-like grip.

'Now we'll play "Murder in the Dark",' said Llewelyn.

As the curtains were drawn, we saw Clive and Eira climbing up the veranda steps, just in time to join the game. The rules were explained to Booda by a series of tableaux. I hoped I'd be victim first. The detective whose job it was to find the murderer failed to declare himself. It turned out to be Booda, who had wanted to be the murderer. The cards were shuffled again. I was the detective and left the room. The noise of bumps and shrieks from the room only stopped when the curtains were pulled back and the detective was called to view the body – Llewelyn. Shelagh, Dolly, Desmond, Eira, Clive and Booda all looked guilty. I asked a few questions, prompted by the dead boy who suggested better ones. The murderer turned out to be Shelagh.

'Quick, quick,' said Desmond, trying to make an undetected exit. 'Mrs Dylan's back!'

We all looked up, but Llewelyn decreed we could have one more game if we played quietly. Booda was the murderer and everyone got on their knees to be out of his reach. Booda pulled up a victim from the floor, whooping in delight, while Llewelyn started shouting to restore order. Dad put his head round the door.

'Cat,' he called, as she burst into the room. Dad watched quietly, with a faint smile.

I explained the game to him when he was installed with a beer in his hand waiting for his lunch, delicious stew smells wafting from the kitchen. He said he wasn't allowed to play such games in Cwmdonkin as his father was very sensitive to noise.

'He spent his time at home in his study.'

'We can only play when you and Mum are out,' I explained, 'and Llewelyn's home. He knows the rules to all of the games.'

Dad wanted to know about Booda. 'How can a deaf and dumb man be blind man, too?' he asked.

'That's half the fun,' I admitted. 'Booda wants to know when he can play again.'

On Christmas Day, Shelagh and Desmond went back to their own families while Dolly cooked our Christmas lunch. I had seen Shelagh's mother, Kathleen, with her wavy, luxuriant black hair, but never knew where they lived. By listening discreetly, I learnt that Kathleen lived with a man who was not Shelagh's father.

With Desmond and Shelagh away, Llewelyn gave me more attention. When not actually fighting and taunting each other we got on quite well. I found his collections inspiring and wished I could feel so strongly about stamps and birds' eggs and be as diligent in studying and amass-ing them. He kept his eggs collected over the years in a proper show box with indentations for eggs and labels for their names. I occasion-ally borrowed one of the small speckly eggs to amuse Granny but she advised me to return it immediately before it broke.

Seahorses were Llewelyn's latest interest and I was terrified of them. He showed me pictures of a creature with a horse's head and neck and a mermaid-like tail. I was terrified of meeting this fearsome animal in the estuary at high tide, perhaps washed into the garden through the harbour opening. Llewelyn plucked off the wall the tiny seahorse replica made of transparent shell, the material of flotsam and jetsam, waving it in front of my face. 'Want to hold it?' he offered as I cowered.

Later on Christmas morning, Eira and Gwyneth came to collect me for the church service. St Martin's was perched on one of the hills above Laugharne. We walked quickly up the steep incline to the churchyard, filled with headstones draped in ivy and forlorn under dark yews. Walking towards the open church door, I thought of the few sad things that troubled me – a dead cat that the rat-catcher found and quickly hid in the sack with the other poisoned animals and the way Mother sometimes preferred Colm, even though he wasn't a novelty any more. And now, passing under the branches dripping on to the headstones covered with lichen, I thought of all those dead people no one could remember.

I felt a tear trickling down my face which I had to hide as the beaming verger was saying 'Happy Christmas' as if he had invented it. I invited the dead people outside to come in because it was Christmas. I could see them at the back of the congregation, the verger making space for them, the singers moving closer along the pews, cheerfully, without hesitation. Eira had to find my place in the hymnal because all this rearranging of reality was distracting. It was cold but my feet, in wool socks darned by mother in surprising colours, were warm, and there was the prospect of lunch in the dining room, with the coal fire and playing games with my father after-wards.

Someone had decked whole branches of holly around the altar and on every available surface. Sprouting from vases and umbrella stands were winter branches of different kinds with little white or black berries, mixed in with chrysanthemums which gave a splash of colour to all the greenery. Advent candles decked the altar, giving the ill-lit church a welcoming glow.

We started with a rousing hymn which we attacked with gusto. A man with a big voice shouted even louder than normal but he was far enough away not to drown us out. The congregation were spread out, with spaces left as usual in the front pews where no one wanted to sit too near the proceedings and the beady eye of the vicar who noticed every yawn and commented on them after the service as we trooped out to where he waited at the door.

The service went much as it always did on Sunday, though more people had come to pay their Christmas respects and give a donation to the Christmas collection for the orphans at our local orphanage. I saw Eira put a button and a penny in the collection which I quizzed her on when another hymn started up.

'I was hoping the silver button off my blazer might make more noise and seem like more money.' she hissed loud enough over the hymn but still in a whisper. 'I forgot to ask my mother for sixpence.' She added, 'It was my spare button.'

Christmas Day meant that all the women wore their moth-eaten furs which helped keep them warm on such a miserable day – colder in the church than out. Everyone wore hats except children like us. Mother had tried to make me wear a tam o' shanter that Granny had given me for a birthday or some celebration, which I removed as soon as I could.

The vicar was climbing up to his pulpit for his address. He then proceeded to reprimand all the people who were there but were not regular church-goers. It occurred to me that this might not encourage them to return another time. Scripture readings were dispatched by the church warden who delivered them with extra gusto and those napping at the back were temporarily woken by his deep and urgent delivery of the psalms and New Testament readings.

After Communion, the choir (a motley collection of maiden aunts, boys with soprano voices and one lone man growling in the background) sang the festive anthem. Some of the congregation couldn't resist joining in despite the warning looks of the vicar. I was rather hoping Big Voice might disrupt the proceedings further but he preserved his voice for the remaining hymn which was a carol: 'Oh Come All Ye Faithful'.

We came out of the church into a cold day, our breath making swirls in the air. The walk back under the weeping trees and the low-lying estuary mists failed to make me gloomy again. We met Mother coming the other way to meet me and we walked back together.

The woodwork of the dining room was painted in a high-gloss liver-brown as Mother called it, the sideboard a bright sky-blue. Mother was for bright colour against a neutral background, with coloured prints, shawls and Welsh honeycomb bedspreads. The sideboard and window ledges, fireplace and skirting had the same shiny brown as the woodwork on the outside of the house. The writing shed was painted green.

In the grate hung huge swathes of holly, singed at the edges, with holly also peeping out from behind jugs and seasonal plates on the sideboard. Mistletoe was hung from the corners of the reproductions of Renoir, Matisse and Dutch interiors. Renoir's bonneted children looked like me when I was young, Mother said. Dolly kept winking as she pointed at the mistletoe.

'Better keep Clive away, might get ideas.' My cheeks were becoming redder and Mother told me not to go so near the hot coals.

Dolly was cooking lunch and delicious roast smells came from the kitchen.

'Your father will be here soon,' said Mother.

She was ready for lunch, having walked around the village before meeting me. She kept running upstairs to see whether Dylan was back; on Christmas Day, he kept to routine. I followed her to the front door to see his portly figure swaying down the path. He was accompanied by one of the Williams' brothers, a set of strong shoulders and a lean body, carrying a doll's house. My father was veering towards the cliff.

'Look out!' I shouted as the doll's house swayed and the Williams' brother pulled my father back from the brink. My moment of surprise and triumph was overwhelming and I burst into tears. My brother looked disgusted, knowing the doll's house, made lovingly by a local carpenter, could only be for me. This was the one he threw over the cliff later after one of our disagreements. But we all admired the wooden house and its contents, and I settled down to put them in order, moving wardrobes from the bathroom and the kitchen chairs from the bedrooms.

It was time for lunch. On the table set with a white Granny table-cloth, with lace inlay on the four corners, was a turkey on a thick oblong serving dish with a blue and white pattern. Around this centre-piece were serving dishes of mashed potato, swede, sprouts and roast potatoes sprigged with thyme from the garden. I can't remember if my grandparents were there for the feast. In my mind, they fitted best in their own home and made no impression on Christmas Day, not least because my father was – unusually – eating with us.

Christmas pudding must have followed, with custard, everyone's favourite. We pulled cheap crackers, plastic prizes falling out on the floor. My father invited us to guess what the object might be: a cockroach, a submarine or a liner.

'A fish,' I suggested.

No one agreed. It was a Phoenix or bird of unknown species, my father said with authority. We couldn't really understand the jokes, though clever Llewelyn said the riddles were easy once you had the answer. Only my father and Llewelyn attempted sensible answers.

'Where do fish keep their money?'

'In a fishy wallet made of seaweed,' I offered.

The answer 'In a river bank' was beyond me. My father explained the double meaning. Why did everyone groan at the answer? I imagined a special bank for fishes and thought of *The Wind in the Willows* where Toad could drop in to cash a cheque for the car or caravan which he'd crash and reduce to smithereens. I was told to 'wake up': Llewelyn hated people not concentrating on games.

Then it was time for games chosen by my father. Mother was told to stop fighting with the crate which had arrived the previous week, a present from a friend in America, its contents unknown. She showed her injured hand and shouted to Dolly to find a hammer. We could not start our game of Charades while Mother pitted her will and strength against the unyielding boards. The sharp edge of the hammer was used, Mother's foot against the crate. It suddenly ceded with a splintering noise, Mother fell down but nothing fell out except shredded

Dylan at home with Caitlin, Aeron, Colm and Mably.

paper. We were waiting for something extraordinary to appear but dried fruit was just as good. It was the first time I had eaten a dried fig and, though it was hard, it tasted sweet and strange.

'Could I go first for Charades?' I begged, as Mother brought armfuls of costumes and hats from her store. Llewelyn objected and someone else began. I can only remember what I mimed: the words spaghetti and macaroni, syllable by syllable, as I put on a different hat for every scene. Everyone poked fun at everyone else's turn. I put a homburg on as I mimed 'spa', and imagined walking down the quay of some sea village and having a dip in the sea. Everyone explained that spa waters are usually spring waters. They all knew my words from the beginning as I chose the same ones every year.

'I wore a hat,' I explained, 'because there was a cold sea breeze.'

We opened our presents during the afternoon. I got books from my parents, and chocolates from Granny, which made Mum pull a disapproving face. My father started to read my books to himself: *Mary Poppins*, *The Secret of Spiggy Holes* and school stories by Angela Brazil.

As the afternoon drew on, we played Noughts and Crosses and Hangman, munching sweets and drinking pop. It was getting hot in the small room with the heavy scent of leftovers, dried fruit and singed holly, and time for my father to leave for the Brown's for a sociable drink. I was full and tired. When I started pulling things out from my morning Christmas stocking, finding my tin trumpet, I saw my father move restlessly in his chair. I played the trumpet as loudly as I could and a thin whistle sound limped out . . . but it was enough. My mother told us to get ready for bed. What, so early? Yes, tonight she was going out, too.

Before bed I went outside. The tide was creeping through the square hole in the garden wall and I rushed out on to the veranda to look down on the waters half-filling the garden at that time of year. Putting the tin whistle trumpet to my lips, I gave a Christmas greeting. A thin moon cast its pale beams on the estuary. As the tide came in, water rapidly cast its circle ever wider. The light from the sky painted silvery grey patches, which eddied towards our wall, entering the harbour like a determined but not unwelcome guest. Our lights and the moon made the rapidly filling pool of our back garden strange and eerie but not frightening at all.

I shivered in the cold night air as Mother called me to go up the steps to the house and to bed, so I went upstairs and pulled out my favourite book to finish off a perfect day – Mary Poppins gripping her magic carpet bag and holding her hat in place with her hand and hat pin. I was not allowed to disturb Colm by switching on the light, so I fumbled for the torch under my pillow. Before I found it, I fell asleep.

After Christmas

B y Boxing Day, I already wanted to see Shelagh but she only appeared a week after the festivities. Once she came into the kitchen, I explained that the stew on the stove in the large black pot was not for us but for my mother to feed to my dad, however tempting it smelt. Mother had thrown away the last one and started afresh, with bones, leeks, turnips, potatoes, carrots, cabbage leaves minimally chopped, salt and pepper. This would simmer and cook for a week, and have more vegetables and potatoes added until it changed colour, merging from brown to green.

We exchanged news about our presents. I told Shelagh I had asked for a cat but that mother disliked cats more than rats. I told her about the cat poisoned by mistake by the rat-man, and how we'd dropped it in the sack with the corpses of rats and it was a secret.

There was also time to see Granny and Grandpa after the festivities with a string bag containing all my presents, which were unpacked by me with much commentary. I took a sample of every dried fruit taken from the broken Californian crate for tasting. But Granny said they'd break her teeth unless she soaked them overnight.

'I must tell my mother,' I said. 'She makes us eat them hard.'

At the mention of my mother, Granny said not to bother. She probably had stronger teeth than Grandpa and her. I thought to myself, 'That's someone else frightened of her.'

The next day Mother beat me on the bottom for some disgrace or other. I then fled to Granny's, who had opened the door and took me into her arms.

'Now, now, don't be upsetting yourself,' she consoled. 'You stay here tonight. I'll tell Daddy you're here to look after me.' She said, 'She's got a terrible temper. She can't help it.'

I dried my face with Grandpa's hanky, and Granny left me alone. I threw a tennis ball savagely against the lavatory door and was surprised when my grandfather appeared with a large book in his hand, picked up the ball and threw it back to me with his free hand. He was a very educated man, Granny always said, never without a book in his hand.

I returned indoors dry-eyed, distracted by Grandpa's sudden appearance. We did some drawing, first cows and sheep, then our boat, the Cuckoo, but Granny thought it was a gate in the cows' field. I copied her boat which looked more like a gate than my own. At supper, D.J. came out of the study with his hat on, looking aloof and indifferent. He never fussed over me when Granny was there.

That day, Dad came to visit the Pelican on his way to the Brown's.

'Is Aeron here?' he asked Grandpa. 'Cat says she has to go home now.'

I ran to him, 'Can I stay here?'

'Yes, Cat said she could stay, if Granny didn't mind,'

'Dad,' I wheedled, 'she beat me,' and pulled down my knickers to show the marks. 'She always beats me on my bum,' I explained. Grandpa looked appalled and made me pull them up again.

'Never mind,' said Dad, putting his hand on my shoulder. 'You stay here till your mum calms down.' Dad was much nicer than Mum, I told Granny when my father went into Grandpa's room for a chat.

'Now, now,' she said, not taking sides.

Aeron and Granny Flo in bed. (Photo courtesy of Rollie McKenna).

We were sitting in Granny's bed the day after the rift, discussing the new words I should not use. At my insistence, Granny's presents lay all over the bed. A jumbo tin of chocolate powder was included amongst the glass jars of bath salts and boxes of sweets with liquid centres. I eyed them with interest. There were two packages with

unopened Christmas wrapping of Santa dressed in red with his rein-
deer, their antlers the same red.

'I saved these to open last,' she said. 'I was so busy Christmas Day
seeing to the lunch as we'd invited Gwen from next door and we couldn't
leave out her husband who never says a word and when I found out
her son was visiting and would be coming too with his fiancée I
wondered what I'd got myself into . . .' said Granny in one breath.

Then, without a pause, she continued lecturing me about forbidden words that you hear from 'them up in the Estate but shouldn't
use yourself'.

'It's not nice to say "bastard",' said Granny. 'Only people we don't
like say that.'

'But Mother said "you bastard" to Dad, when they were shouting
at each other,' I objected. But Granny would make no exceptions, and
said I mustn't repeat naughty words, whoever said them. It was all
confusing.

I would ask Mother how you got babies and she always answered.
The answer was what Granny called 'not nice' and I did not believe
Mother. Given a graphic description of Colm's birth, every scream
and pain recorded, I would not listen. How could babies come out
covered in blood and from where precisely? It could be the belly
button which I'd learned was where sex took place. Perhaps she was
inventing such things to compensate for Colm being the favourite
but I was not fooled. I told Granny and she said that Mother shouldn't
be frightening me and changed the subject. But she never criticized
Mother to me even when she disagreed with her.

I told Granny the f-word Clive had told me, but it gave her a chance
to warn me against him. He was not clean enough for her.

'That reminds me,' she said, picking up the newspaper, 'after a little read, I'm going to scrub your neck at the back.'

'What about "For Christ's sake"? Is that naughty?' I asked, still occupied by swearwords. 'Mummy said that when Dad said something Mummy didn't like . . . I forget what.'

'Just close your ears,' advised Granny.

'And wash your mouth out,' I added.

'Yes,' she agreed.

I snuggled into her side, the two hollows of the soft mattress became one, and she wasn't cross anymore as she turned the large sheets of newspaper, one sheet my side. I read the headlines, inhaled Granny's dry biscuit smell, and thought of nothing except being safe there in the bed with someone who knew I was special. Perhaps I could move in. Mother would be pleased to be rid of me.

A ring at the door broke into our world. A bad-tempered Grandpa could be heard muttering and opening the door. A few words and there was Mother like a golden sun beaming.

'I'll come and get you before lunch,' she said, 'unless you want to stay with Granny.' Disloyally, I agreed to be ready. I had to contain myself not to ask to go immediately. I padded after Mother and she ruffled my hair fondly, yesterday's harsh words and deeds forgotten. 'You can help me tidy the shed.'

Dad didn't take time off from his work routine unless ill or away so on Boxing Day his routine returned to normal.

In the morning he went to the Brown's Hotel to drink and do the crossword or place small bets on the horses. On one such occasion he wrote a postcard to a friend – which I still have:

Running Water and Nuts
French Bounty and Knuckles
D'Angelo and Chammie
Belby, Belby, Belby
Jackmill and Ambiguity
are some of the camels we have mounted.

While he was betting, talking, listening and drinking, Mother and I tidied his shed. One day she lit the paraffin-fuelled stove as usual while he was out so that it was warm and snug for the afternoon's session. I was told to pick up the two Penguin paperbacks from the rough kitchen table, which served as his desk. There was an Agatha Christie and a Raymond Chandler.

'Hide them,' Mother said, so I tucked them behind books on the heavy bookshelf but I'd tell him later where to find them.

My mother had drawing pins and a *Picture Post* with her and pulled out the centrefold: a reproduction of Bruegel the Elder's *Peasant Wedding*. I helped Mother pin the shiny picture on the boards of the shed wall next to the portraits of Walt Whitman and D.H. Lawrence. My mother said Dad didn't look at anything when he worked except the estuary and the hills on the other side. It was she who arranged to have the two windows installed into the old garage to make a workplace for him, she told me. He did not need to look at the pictures on the walls.

The view inspired many word pictures: 'Poem in October', 'Poem on his Birthday', 'Over Sir John's Hill' and the unfinished, 'In Country Heaven'. The poems record curlews, herons, hawks, cormorants and oyster-catchers, but not the fishing boat at full tide, though

Pictures on the wall in Dylan's shed.

it makes an appearance in *Under Milk Wood*. Mother said I was very good at advising where to place the pictures in the shed and holding the drawing pins. After this praise, I loved her again, even more than Dad.

His interest in pictures was minimal. He never commented on the illustrations of lonely forests in Grimms' sombre fairy tales or Arthur Rackham's skeletal, winter trees and roots in *The Wind in the Willows*. He seemed to prefer imagining the scenes as he read them. I would often stop him reading to me and ask where the nice lady who lived in the sweet-house was hiding, or where the woodchopper was waiting to save the day. He would tear open his box of Woodbines to draw a sketch of the action.

Once with a great deal of puffing and grunting, he rearranged the furniture in the sitting room so that scuttle, armchair and footrest marked Hansel and Gretel's sweet-house, the mound of leaves where they rested, and the cauldron where they were nearly boiled. He used cushions to add sheds and an outside privy. He knew a lot more about the story than the illustrator, I concluded.

Birthday Parties

The festivities of Christmas were long gone but children's parties took place all year round – often lasting overnight as the children piled into an oversize bed and into the next day with extended games away from the house where the first party had taken place. It was only the neglected child who couldn't persuade their parents to put on a splash for their little friends. The child with the nearest birthday would milk the situation to bursting point in the playground, promising to invite a particular person, then taking them off the list if they quarrelled. The primary school was always abuzz with the next birthday bash.

In February I was returning one Saturday from a birthday party in Orchard Park in a disgruntled mood: the parents of the party had insisted we go home before dark. I met Idris on the square, who invited me to his own party. Not being one of his special friends –

which he'd made quite sure I knew during school when he told everyone out loud his wish list – I was surprised to be accosted and invited. He was rather a grubby boy and Granny would have disapproved but I accepted instantly as my friends Eira and Gwyneth were going and I'd be able to tell everyone about going to yet another party, proving my popularity. I didn't know what my mother would say, having to find another birthday present so soon. My mother seem somewhat distracted when I told her and said I could take one of Llewelyn's albums, given to him at Christmas, which he said he already had.

Idris was celebrating his seventh birthday with ten of his best friends. The usual sweet dishes for Sunday teas were laid out on a white tablecloth. The glass-cut bowls from the seldom-disturbed sideboard held red, orange and green jellies and pink and yellow blancmange. Balloons were tied to each chair to be taken home at the end. Thinly cut meat paste or Marmite sandwiches were banked on dinner plates and I was glad to see crustless Spam sandwiches not far from me.

Idris, at the top of the table, wore a grin of triumph as he surveyed the glorious display, his unopened presents beside him. My present was at the bottom to hide the battered tissue paper, elastic band and loosely tied bright hair ribbon. The birthday boy looked unusually clean, his knees and elbows scuffed but pink and not streaked with dirt. His short trousers, white shirt and laced shoes were new. Some pitying relative had probably bought shoes and clothes as a birthday present.

The orangeade and pop were poured into our glasses, their vivid colour competing with the jellies. Anything that looked different from

the drab food we ate everyday – even the mouse-colour welsh-cakes
– gave us a sense of occasion.

I started with sandwiches washed down with pop to prolong the
moment before we plunged into the sweet stuff. The hovering aunts
(some of them neighbours and friends who we called auntie) passed
the plates of sandwiches from which you were expected to take exactly
two half rounds . . . more to be given on a second round. Then it
was time for jelly and it seemed a shame to wreck the perfect
puddings, ladled out trembling into our small bowls, the colour glow-
ing through the glass. We waited for Birthday Boy's mother to say
'Go to it, now.'

When we could eat no more, the presents were unwrapped. Mine
had dropped its ribbon before the unveiling but was well received: a
bumper comic annual. Following the party custom, it was then time
to play games.

As we sat on the carpet passing the parcel, my school friend, Eira,
whispered in my ear that the cousins were going after tea. That was
good . . . I had optimistically told my mother not to expect me back
as I wanted to stay the night after the party. Mother ignored Dolly's
criticism of Idris' family as Dolly knew something disgraceful about
most people in Laugharne. Supposedly, Idris' uncle was having it off
with his mother (what did that mean precisely?) while his dad was
down the pub every night.

Then the cake arrived: a round home-made confection smothered
in Smarties. Idris blew at the candles but dislodged half a dozen sweets
without extinguishing the feeble flames. In exasperation, his older
brother blew out the lot, depositing spit over the Smarties, grabbing
at the ones that had fallen, stuffing them in his mouth and starting

a quarrel. I would keep my slice till later, I decided. After another drink, we settled down to quiet games: snakes and ladders as well as snap and other card games. Nothing was said but at bedtime we took off our dresses and shoes and joined Idris and his young cousins in the huge matrimonial bed, vacated for one night. We threw around a few pillows and bolsters before the grown-ups objected and then were forced to settle down. Some of us were on the top end of the bed, the others made to sleep at the foot end. The girls somehow were relegated to the lower end and had to fight to gain one of the pillows for ourselves. This brought Idris' mother upstairs who threatened to evict us if we didn't go to sleep nicely.

That night, every time we moved, Idris claimed we were hurting his bad knee. He was still taking advantage of being Birthday Boy and sent one of his little cousins to join the girls at the bottom of the bed, taking pity on him by giving him an extra pillow. In the silence that followed, he complained that his auntie hadn't given him a proper present, only new shoes. We felt the indignity, but didn't give him the satisfaction by saying so. Though we were annoyed to have so little room, it was companionable to 'cwch' (Welsh for hug). Before being able to fully enjoy the novelty of seven in a bed, I fell asleep as soundly and heavily as a log.

Returning home the next day from my little holiday, I went to call on Granny. Disturbed from the housework she liked to finish in the morning, she was not in her best mood. 'Been catching nits!' she exclaimed as she polished with one of the velvet bags I had helped sew. 'We've only just got rid of the last lot. Lucky I've still got the comb.'

She also told me that Margaret Taylor, my father's patroness and payer of bills, had arrived that morning. Before I could rush off to see her, Granny managed to fit in a few more grumbles at the crumpled state of my party dress and my scuffed shoes. She had stopped rubbing the furniture, so I left before she could think up something else against the family at Orchard Park, a council estate, as Granny never failed to point out.

There was little time to pause but the estuary was sparkling with reflected sunlight and the primroses were just showing their heads in the hedgerows. Then, I saw Margaret looking the way Mother never would: smart, conventional and, best of all, unobtrusive in eggshell colours of creams and browns, just turning by the garden gate on to the cliffwalk. Her hair was long and brown in contrast to mother's wild fairness. She wore a smart woollen suit nipped in at the waist, fitting snugly over her ample hips and falling into folds of heavy material for such a spring-like day, in which the sun warmed the still cold air. Stockings covered her legs and lacy gloves her hands, which clutched the handles of a box-shaped leather handbag. Mother followed bare-legged and sandalled, swinging a basket.

Margaret was very fond of me, and was one of those women who exuded warmth and enthusiasm. My mother often criticized her for 'gushing': 'Not everything is "lovely, Ducky", she mimicked unkindly. 'In fact life's bloody awful most of the time.' But I liked Margaret for her boundlessly positive attitude. She made the best of everything, and made everything more fun for us children. I remembered staying with her in Oxford and became her third daughter, only to be reminded painfully that I was a 'Thomas' on leaving.

That night my parents went to the pub, taking Margaret with them. Now she was in Laugharne she did what my parents did without changing the routine. She joined my father in his morning session at the pub and both my parents in the evenings. The routine was made more interesting for her visits, however, because the locals were invited back for more drinking and carousing.

That first evening, long after I had gone to bed, Mother crashed through the bedroom door and the sounds of conviviality downstairs came with her. The baby groaned slightly and rolled over in his sleep.

'Leave Colm alone,' I said protectively, but she ignored my warning and looked at me fondly, bending over to breathe alcohol all over me. Colm was disturbed by the mention of his name and snuffled but did not wake.

When she left, I crept down to have a look. Through the door left carelessly ajar, I saw Crossmouse and his cronies starting to sing drunkenly. Neither my mother nor my father was keen on singing, preferring talking or dancing. You could hear Mother cranking up the gramophone and I thought, 'Look out.' *Swan Lake*'s overture was turned up to spoil the imperfect harmony, and Mother was leaping around so embarrassingly that even Margaret told her she'd hurt herself.

'Fuck you,' answered Mother as she went out, slamming the front door.

I crept back upstairs to my bedroom from my vantage point viewing the proceedings downstairs and did not dare to look through my bedroom window to see what she was doing outside. Colm's breathing became quicker but he slept on. I didn't want to see Mother cart-wheeling on the front lawn and showing her knickers to all those men (who were probably looking out of the sitting room window to get an eyeful) but the picture in my mind was so awful I decided to look to get it over. She was all on her own sitting on the lawn outside the front door rolling a cigarette.

When Margaret stayed, my father was forced to share his work time with her as well as the pub crawls, and she was sometimes even allowed in his writing shed when he should have been working. On my return from school one day, they were missing and I was sent to spy on them. I searched all over Laugharne, with instructions to tell Father to get back to work, and I prepared my defence. I was on my way to the shops, perhaps, or looking for Margaret to talk about her daughters. As I bent to look through the shed keyhole my bottom was playfully smacked.

'We're here,' said Margaret. 'We've been for a stroll'.

I was outraged on my mother's behalf. The afternoons were for writing and my father never went for a stroll except to the pub. Margaret realized that I was displeased.

'Come along, we have lots to talk about. We'll leave your dad. He has things to do.'

He disappeared into his shed. Mother would be happy he was back at work, I thought. But he spoilt it by reappearing like a rabbit from a conjurer's hat, saying, before he vanished again, 'See you and Cat later.'

'And me,' I added.

'And you,' Dad smiled at me. 'Now you tell your mum I'm not to be disturbed.' What he meant was Margaret, not Mum, of course.

'Yes, Dad,' I said, avoiding a wink of complicity. 'I can show you the ruins,' I said to her.

Margaret and I walked along the cliffwalk, to the ruined cottages.

The overhang of trees and bushes, with lacy branches showing their buds ready to spring green, filtered the sunlight on the dried mud path. Margaret did not seem to appreciate the beauties of nature. She was wearing sandals with red socks instead of her usual brogues or her smart travelling outfit of high heels, suit and hat – a dressmaker's imitation of what Mother and I studied in the glossy magazines.

The sandals and socks were Margaret's attempt at Mother's unique style, so Mother said, 'Though she never gets it quite right.' Dolly asked me if all mother's friends wore socks. In Oxford Margaret sometimes wore Mother's style of striped cotton skirts and Mother complained about being copied. Margaret also fussed with the floral chiffon head-scarf, which was not Mother's style.

'The girls are always asking about you,' she said. 'They say they miss your games. What's the carpet game they keep talking about?'

'Oh, that,' I said. 'Can't remember exactly.' I remembered it exactly as I could recall the time before Laugharne when I visited Oxford and the Taylors for weeks on end at the ages of four and five and even younger.

My memories of the immediate post-war years of Oxford are mainly domestic ones. I shared a bedroom with Sophia and Amelia, both younger than I was. At breakfast, their father, Alan, held a debating chamber with his two sons, Giles and Sebastian, both immeasurably more mature than us. A.J.P. introduced a political topic and the boys were encouraged to take opposing views. We were not allowed to leave the table until, looking at his watch, A.J.P. dismissed us all to leave for his 9 o'clock lecture, so early that some students turned up in their pyjamas.

One memorable day Margaret took me into Oxford on the back of her bike. This time the girls were left with my mother who was cooking a stew, the pig's ears sticking out from the top of the pan. A woman waved to me and I grandly waved back from my vantage point. A bus-driver hooted and Margaret and I waved back to him. When a boy pulling up his socks looked up at us, we both stuck out our tongues at him at the same moment and giggled. He ran along the pavement to show that running was quicker than peddling and tripped on his laces.

I told Dad about it later when we were taking a walk along the river, stopping to look at the weir which rushed past the house. In silence we both watched the gushing water with appreciation. He finally broke the spell, saying he'd have done the same.

'You'd have got stuck in the seat,' I said.

'And then I'd have to go round and round Oxford on the back of Margaret's bike for ever,' he agreed. Suddenly remembering, he said, 'I have to get back. Cat has cooked a new stew.'

I told him about the pig's ears and he laughed, miming a pig's ears with whiskery tufts.

But the visit to Oxford ended badly. Mother complained about Alan's 'meanness' because he hid the bottles when the Thomases appeared and consumed the children's free government rations of malt, cod liver oil and orange juice, adding gin to the latter. The antagonism between A.J.P. and the Thomases grew worse as we stayed on and on. During their stay, my parents made friends with Ernest and Kathleen Stahl as well as A.L. Rowse. Stephen Spender and his wife were also often guests at the Taylors. Though he was never unkind to me, a cuckoo in the nest, A.J.P. was always distant, as he was with his own daughters. One day I met my father grumbling to himself by the vegetable patch he tended to favour.

'What are you doing?' he asked me distractedly as if I'd appeared from the ground like a radish.

'It's me,' I reminded him. 'I was looking for Amelia.'

'You can go back to your mother, now,' he said. 'I'm going into my caravan in a minute. Tell me about the games you play with the girls?' he asked, suddenly interested in his own train of thought.

'Run and catch and skipping, but not with the boys. They're rough.' He looked at me as if I was saying the most interesting things in the world. 'I can push Amelia over,' I said to keep the momentum of his interest. 'Sometimes she pushes me over.'

'I haven't seen you skipping,' he said.

That was a sore point. My arms and legs did not move naturally but got in the way when I tried. We walked to the river and he picked up a stick to poke the weed about. I threw a stone and bubbles appeared in the water. Had I disturbed a fish, we wondered, peering into the green depths. He put his hand briefly on my shoulders.

Margaret's visit to Laugharne brought it all back to me: the girls, the boys and conversations with Dad.

Invitation to America

When John Malcolm Brinnin's invitation to America arrived the very month we were settling into the Boat House at Laugharne, Mother did not immediately sense the dangers such a trip would create. Not only would the temptations be greater but the stresses of separation would prove irreparable.

'People thought our rows meant our marriage was over,' declared Mother to me later. 'When we were screaming at each other and I was accusing him of infidelities, I thought so too. We were both surprised when we managed to make up afterwards.'

Bitter fights in which Mother lashed out physically and verbally, with my father protesting his innocence, followed by reconciliation was the pattern of their life together. As a child, I never felt threatened by their scraps, usually heard at a distance, and it was only after my father's long trips to the United States that I felt a new, sinister atmosphere enter the house. The battles seemed more earnest and more public, taking place in front of me and Dolly or anyone else who happened to be around. The silences between them were worse than the rows.

It seemed that writing and touring were not possible for my father. On his visits abroad – Prague, Persia and especially America – my father was not either willing or able to write anything. When he went with the family to Italy for three months in 1947, he found even the hours left alone to write in a peasant's cottage near Florence not as satisfactory as living in Wales and following the routine set up by Mother. He only managed one rather atypical poem influenced by fairy tales and his recent memories of the cool green countryside of Llangain and Laugharne, in contrast to the harsher Italian colours and heat. Florence was not Swansea, Laugharne or London. But he was there for poetry and he would write one poem in spite of the heat and homesickness.

Mother loved basking in the sun, and the attention of the young Italian men, often pinching her bottom if close enough. She blossomed while I suffered embarrassment and horror. Dad pined for Wales.

The holiday was subsidized by the scholarship fund of the Society of Authors. My father would have chosen America but the chairman, Edith Sitwell, insisted on Italy. It was also Mother's first choice. She thought America a bad place for someone who drank, and not a place to be poor. The idea behind the award was to give writers an opportunity to write or recover from writing and my father planned to write poetry as a change from his film scripts.

He wrote tempting letters to friends, inviting them to stay and share the delights, but only a few of their friends could afford holidays abroad. The McAlpines and John Davenport accepted but subsequently had to decline. Mother was disappointed that Helen McAlpine couldn't come. Mother said Dylan felt isolated amongst foreigners while the rest of us made the best of the rare holiday.

I have strong memories of the luxurious villa, with a swimming pool, shuttered windows and a garden with cactus bushes, pines and olive trees. My father described it to Margaret Taylor: 'The pooled ponded rosed goldfished arboured lizarded swinghung towelled winetabled Aeronshrill garden leads into our own (dear God) olives and vines climbing to a mutes' conventicle, Niobe's eisteddfod, of cypresses.' More prosaically, he wrote to his parents: 'It's on the hills above Florence, some five miles away or more from the centre, from the great Cathedral dome which we can see from the sunbathing terrace above our swimming-pool. It's a very big villa, with huge rooms and lovely grounds, arbours, terraces, pools; we have a pinewood and a vineyard of our own.

I took advantage of being ignored for once, and ventured alone past the heavy wrought-iron gates. The grass grew above my waist on either side of the earth-beaten drive and I gazed at the profusion of poppies firing the dry grass and licking the path. The sun beat down on my head and I felt alone and triumphant. Another time I clambered between the cacti, fleshy leaves grazing my legs with their thorns, as I made my way to the hut with glass windows. But then, bellowing with indignation, I felt the thorns bite into my skin. My screams alerted my father, who lumbered out to save me. He groaned and staggered, wheezing, holding on to me for grim life, then collapsed into a deckchair. My mother and Aunt Brigit appeared and my thorns were extracted. I screamed again as Brigit skilfully used a needle scorched by a match.

'You shouldn't disturb your father,' Mother said 'You know he doesn't like your noise.'

I was only grateful to be saved. As a result of the cactus episode and other interruptions, my father organized somewhere else to write: a cottage on the estate where he could be cool, with closed shutters. It was difficult to tell whether he loathed the noise of children playing more than the sun. He wrote about both. To John Davenport he wrote: 'Our little spankers make so much noise I cannot work anywhere near them, God grenade them.' And referring to a notorious murderer of the time, 'Aeron's making a noise like a female parrot locked in a room with Heath'. 'Children would turn paradise into a menagerie,' he wrote to Donald Taylor. Yet despite the distractions, by August he had completed 'In Country Sleep', his only poem to me.

Visit to America

M y father flew out to New York on 20 February 1950, to return
by sea on the *Queen Elizabeth* on 1 June that same year, after
a gruelling lecture tour of the United States and Canada. This tour
was arranged by John Malcolm Brinnin with little expertise. Originally,
Brinnin had intended to tempt my father over to the United States
for a single reading at the Young Men's and Women's Hebrew
Association (YM-YWHA) Poetry Center, of which Brinnin was the
new director. Eventually, my father hoped for a post at an American
university. He nearly succeeded, but came to be seen as unreliable,
though he only failed to appear at one of his thirty-nine public readings in the United States and Canada. Because of his drinking at
faculty parties his reputation for outrageous behaviour preceded him
throughout the tour, to the delight of press and public.

At the beginning, I felt upset with his absence. I felt proud that
my father could be so in demand that he travelled that far and, to
believe Mother, was given such importance.

This she said with both pride and bitterness. As the months went
on, Mother and I nonetheless settled into a routine which much of the
time banished even thoughts of my father. In Mother's case, she seemed
happier as the weather grew warmer, reminding her that Dylan would
be back. Sometimes she complained to friends, who became more plen-
tiful as the summer arrived, that Dylan was obviously enjoying himself
while she was left in the bogs with the children and that bloody dog.

While in America, my father made contact with old friends and
acquaintances as well as strangers. These included Henry Miller

whom he greatly admired. He knew Miller's *Tropic of Cancer* and called it the 'best fucking book' ever written. When he lent his copy of Miller's book to Ivy Williams, the landlady of the Brown's Hotel, she was forced to hide the book in the oven in case her husband, Ebi, found it.

On his first tour he wailed to Caitlin that the money intended for home had vanished into travel and living expenses. 'I'm just a voice on wheels. And the damnest thing is that quite likely I may arrive home with hardly any money at all, both the United States <u>and</u> Great Britain taxing my earnings – my earnings for us, Colm, Aeron, Llewelyn, for our house that makes me cry to think of, for the water, the heron, old sad empty Brown's.'

In his letters, I was referred to as 'sweet fiend Aeron' and 'arrant Aeron', while Colm the golden was 'my beloved Colm'. 'I want to live quietly, with you & Colm, & noisily with Aeronwy, & I want to see Llewelyn,' he wrote and said he had sent 'lots of chocolates, sweets, & candies, for you, for Aeron, for my mother.'

He apologized for not doing anything more for my birthday. Mother later conceded that he was genuinely homesick on that trip, thinking of Laugharne and family, lonely in spite of parties held in his honour.

His love letters from America were as passionate as ever, a surprise, as they were written by a man who was forming a relationship with other women. He declared: 'I love you, my dear golden Caitlin, profoundly and truly for ever.' I still feel indignant on my mother's behalf. Before she knew about his infidelities, when he first returned from the United States, the conquering hero, she seemed very happy.

While my father was away in America, Mother and I continued the life of home, school and village: walks, classes and trips to Llanmiloe, Carmarthen and Pendine. Mother had introduced me to piano lessons, taught at Pendine; it was a disaster. I preferred painting and drama to dance, the piano and later, the cello. When reading a book, I felt in my element. When curling my fingers to tap the vicarage piano, I was in someone else's territory.

All the furniture was polished to a high sheen, a hazy outline of my face appearing in the upturned piano lid. I made faces but was forced to find a mirror for a better view of my mobile distorted features. When the vicar's wife came in, I pretended a fly had landed in my eye. When she moved towards me, I said I'd got it out and felt my face turning red with embarrassment. Holding my head down so the kind vicar's wife couldn't see my shame, I returned to the keyboard to concentrate on my scales. Tactfully, she disappeared, picking up a tin of Mansion House polish and a rag left behind on the sofa. After piano practice, the vicar's wife invited me to the kitchen for crumpets and tea, the brew so bitter it made me grimace.

Much more to my liking was Friday film night at Llanmiloe Social Club. It was held in a packed medium-sized hall with hard chairs and the screen up front at the top end of the hall. On Friday evenings I waited for the bus with Clive and the gang. We would meet early to visit the sweet-shop, buy pop, liquorice bootlaces, sherbet dabs and hard-boiled sweets striped like tigers, all on tick. 'Put it on the Boat House bill, please,' I'd ask demurely, sometimes successfully.

'You going to the pictures?' we'd ask our school mates.

'My mother won't let me,' was met with derision by those of us with more liberal parents.

'I think it's Roy Rogers this week,' I would say to Clive within earshot of one of the deprived children.

'No, no,' said Clive, with authority, 'It's Laurel and Hardy.'

They were his favourites. Neither of us had any idea what was showing. But the unfortunate offspring of unreasonable parents soon learnt to retaliate: 'I've heard there's no pictures this week. Hall burnt down.' For an awful moment we believed the joker.

'No it hasn't, no it hasn't! When? When? How'd it happen?'

'He's only lying,' said one of our gang, putting us out of our agony.

The anticipation of seeing movies was never quite matched by the event. I had never seen a film before the age of seven but it was heaven to see the madcap antics of Laurel and Hardy, the swashbuckling adventures of Zorro with Senorita waiting to be saved from a burning rooftop, and Tarzan, the apes and pretty young women with fashionable bob hairdos screaming at jungle animals. For the rest of the week, we would gallop like Trigger or take wild leaps, landing on our friends' toes, swinging from tree to tree or horse to roof, colliding into other Tarzans and Zorros. On one occasion a boy borrowed his sister's scarf, wore a Lone Ranger mask and looked for someone who was not already impersonating someone else to play Tonto, his Red Indian friend.

The seats in the improvised cinema were arranged in rows for the occasion and as the children filed in to grab the ones with the best view – or so they imagined – the boys jabbed the girls and other boys smaller than them with their elbows. I always retaliated by pinching any available area of skin, warned by Clive that I'd have my comeuppance. Once in place, everyone forgot their neighbours, craning their heads upwards. As the floor was flat and not stacked for better viewing, the cinema screen was placed high on the wall. The first time I saw moving pictures I felt my jaw slacken with the wonder.

'Did you see that?' I asked Clive as an alien spaceman marched jerkily across the screen.

'It's all right,' he said, 'I seen it before with my Dad in Carmarthen.' For a moment, he gloried in this revelation.

'There's a liar, he is,' opined the boy next to him.

'Shush,' went the entire audience, not wanting to lose a single second of this wonder: not only actors that moved and talked (however indistinctly at times) but with a story to tell and one we wanted to hear and see.

Then, disaster for a few minutes as the reel projected from the back of the hall whirled on itself and the picture disappeared just as the cowboy was sorting out a couple of rogues who, with pistol in hand, were importuning a pretty lady descended by force from the stagecoach. The audience, transported magically to a pioneering America where only the fittest thrived and the Indians better be aware that their country was no longer their own, were suddenly and brutally brought back to reality: a semi-dark hall with rows of children so absorbed by the film they forgot to eat the sweets they'd bought. In the darkness the children vented their frustration on each other, thumping and shouting, until someone in charge stood before them to make an announcement. The film would be starting immediately and we should all settle down.

Those who had moved places to chat or intimidate others all returned to their seats meek as lambs, shushing their neighbours. The film started again with a shudder, skipping the scene we'd been watching and going on to another. There was a rumble of disapproval until one became newly absorbed as the hero was tied up to a tree by a group of desperadoes. Of course we knew he'd escape and only for a moment wondered what had happened to the lady he had so gallantly saved before the unwarranted interruption. Until we came out, blinking into reality, I had forgotten my friends sitting on the hard seats next to me. After the picture show, the driver told us to hurry up or we'd still be there in the morning.

That spring, while Father was away, we also played on the water. The tides were high and flooded our back garden, breaking over the high wall, allowing us to boat in safety. Mother even joined us to dangle her feet over the edge of the Cuckoo, the small rowing boat bought for Colm. One oar was the most I could manage successfully so we went round and round in circles until Colm cried to get out. I used to take pity on him and call Dolly to carry him back to the house, though he didn't deserve it. I had to punish him every so often to redress the balance. The trouble was he was so amenable that I could never give him his just desserts for long.

On one such adventure, I discovered the complete carcass of a sheep washed up on to the Green Banks. It had drifted from the shore opposite, the peninsula which lead to Llanybri and Llangain where the tough but green sea grass grew. The sheep that stayed there were caught very occasionally by the fast incoming spring tides. The sheep's body still had rotting remnants of flesh on the ribcage which formed a cathedral cavity round its chest where seaweed and even crabs and other scuttlies had taken up residence. The head was still intact and the cavities where the eyes once were now housed seaweed washed by the tide twice a day. I returned every day to look at the sheep,

Caitlin and Aeron in the mud with the boat 'Cuckoo'.
(Photo courtesy of Rollie McKenna).

wondering why the farmer and his collie in the farm opposite had failed to save it when he called in all the others at turn of tide. He was the lost sheep of my Bible stories that wasn't found. I took Mother along to see him and asked if Dad would be interested. She stopped to wonder then and said, 'Probably.'

It was festive the day Dad returned to Laugharne. Days before, Dolly and I had stocked up with all his favourite tit-bits, not forgetting the bottled onions and cockles which no one including me was to open and consume beforehand. Mother had been muttering all sorts of threats and grumbles about the Conquering Hero and the Slave at Home and how he'd be lording and bragging to all and sundry. As it happened, he returned looking so dishevelled, obviously very tired and with a racking cough that never seemed to leave him that Mother didn't follow through her threats not to speak to him ever again. She gave him clean clothes and a bath, fed him and took him to Dr Hughes. In a week or two he was transformed and again one of the fold.

The days I waited before pestering him to see my sheep seemed longer as the time went on. A week went by before I let him know, but it was a day or two after that he came with me and said that one day all the drowned fishermen and sheep might walk the mudflats again, wailing and crying like cats. There followed a big discussion about how long the sheep had been there and how many animals could live in the seaweed and froth caught in the skeleton and whether I'd like to draw it. We went for a walk along the shore and up the stone steps to his shed where he disappeared, his muddy shoes leaving footprints. I squelched home with sodden plimsolls drying in the sun.

Dad was exhausted but soon recovered in the fresh sea air, back with his pub, pals and family, and there followed a spate of intense creativity which lasted over the summer. He reapplied himself to *Under Milk Wood*, spouting verses in the bath, and trying them out on Mother. He also wrote new poems, including 'The Author's Prologue' for his *Collected Poems*.

But he had returned with little money and resorted to his begging bowl, writing letters to his usual sponsors. Margaret Taylor was approached for help with bills. 'Oh, ravens, come quick, come quick. Is there any hope? And desperately soon?' He thanked Princess Caetani for a cheque in response to his last financial crisis: 'we can (now) pay some bills, and eat'. He included a newly finished poem, 'Lament', promising others.

Summer Sands

Now Father was back the days grew warmer; summer was approaching and Llewelyn was due to return. With such prospects we planned trips to Pendine Sands, which was the longest stretch of beach for miles around. It was famous as the location for the world speed records attained or attempted by Sir Malcolm Campbell and J.G. Parry-Thomas. It was from there that Amy Johnson and Jim Mollison flew across the Atlantic in 1933. Motorbike championships were also held there regularly. The Ministry of Defence had requisitioned a long section of the sands for the 'Establishment', finding the surface firm enough for heavy army vehicles. Rows of caravans were also along the sands, but even these casually placed eyesores could not detract from the majesty of the bay and headland.

On our outings, often supervised by parents of friends, we would wend our way to the caves under the cliffs, laden with baskets and blankets, through gullies of water, between rocks containing shrimps and miniscule crabs, and past the other summer visitors, praying no one had commandeered our place. In luck, we arranged ourselves at the mouth of the cave – blankets over newspapers to protect the adults from the damp sand, wicker baskets placed on top. A Tizer bottle filled with milk and a butter dish were buried in the cool sand just inside the cave's mouth, the top showing. A square tin box was half buried to keep the cooked meats or cheese fresh. The bread was wrapped in damp tea cloths. Buckets and spades were handed out and we started to put our swimsuits on under dresses or shirts. Whoever was in charge would hold a towel around the girls as we changed into swimsuits so that the boys couldn't see, and then we'd be free to rush, shouting, down to the sea. When the tide was out the waves were not so high and we would find constant joy in jumping over the tame waves, kicking up froth and sand.

Once he had returned from school, Llewelyn would join our trips. Whenever the sun shone, he went with the Evans family, Clem and David, on the bus, to that sandy Shangri-la. One day, I could say proudly that I had been invited by a family who were visiting Laugharne, and with whom I had made friends. Mother was unusually reluctant to let me go as she did not know them but I managed to persuade her.

My first disappointment came when the mother of the family arrived with one string bag and no buckets and spades. Where was the loaf to slice and the breadknife preserved in rolled newspaper for safety? And where was the milk, the tea caddy, the essential camping cooker to boil water? The paraphernalia of our normal outings to Pendine was nowhere to be seen. We motored down the straight coastal road and I missed the fun of the double-decker bus ride. It was already too late to bag a place at the caves so I wasn't surprised when we turned towards the burrows and sand dunes, away from the refreshment kiosk and seaside 'front'. We were so lightly burdened that we seemed to walk easily for miles and then the family settled themselves on towels in a dip between two sand dunes.

My disappointments were soon forgotten when their daughter and I started to explore burrows and dunes, coarse grass growing from the tops, slidy-fine sand hot to the feet and cooler the further down you dug your toes. We were soon absorbed in games, rolling down the dunes, throwing sand until one of us complained about stinging eyes, and generally forgetting how disappointing the day might have been. We were called back for a drink, given some biscuits, and after a break returned to the dunes.

Suddenly, my foot came into contact with something sharp. I looked down, a large piece of white glass from a bottle was stuck into the sole of my foot and when I removed it the bleeding got worse. 'Keep away from there,' I warned my friend and returned to the game. But it was too late – the blood gushed from the wound and I had to present myself to the mother. Her expression was one of surprised anger, not the sympathy which Granny, Mother or Dolly would have offered. Grumbling, she got hold of my shoulder angrily, complaining that I was going to mess up the car, and frog-marched me back along the sands. With a foot beginning to ache as well as bleed I did my best to walk with my good one. The mother shot me a glance of resentment as I hobbled.

I was taken to the surgery at St Clare's, where Dr Hughes gave a running commentary,: 'spoiling the day . . . such a pity', 'such a glorious day if it were not for this'. With no preamble, the doctor dabbed the wound with disinfectant and started to stitch my foot. It felt like the end of the world – worse than the drilling of several dentists as the needle tore through raw flesh. I still have the beautifully executed scar of stitches.

Later that summer the whole family went to Pendine together. This time we were properly laden with baskets and food, though no camp cooker. My special job was to bury Dad's beer in the wet sand where he sat with a straw hat, guarding the cave's entrance.

'Want one yet?' I shouted.

'Make sure it's cold,' said Mother handing Dad a glass tumbler. 'Don't get sand on your father's newspaper,' she said as we raced to the sea and, as we raced back for our picnic, 'Don't get water on your father's newspaper.'

Mably didn't hear, shaking water and sand all over *The Times*. Mother picked him up with one bare foot so that he was suspended for a split second before being deposited slightly further up the beach. In one micro-second, he was back sniffing for food.

In time, Dad asked for a beer and I helped him lever off the top as we lay a sheet of *The Times* under a cloth for his picnic plate. 'It'll get wet,' I said but he'd already read that part, he assured me.

Serving Dad was important work and I made sure Mother did not muscle in; taking small corners off his sandwiches before delivering them – the bread cut by Mother in huge, uneven chunks.

'A mouse been eating the corners?' he asked in amusement, cutting his halves in quarters. 'Come and eat some of mine and sit here,' he said, as a prize for all my hard work.

Leaving my father, pen in hand, scrutinizing the crossword he usually completed with his father in the Brown's, we went to explore the headland. The day was long and summery, my Dad was with us, and everywhere was sand, sand, sand when I was used to mudflats

and rocks. Sand could be dug and fashioned into anything you chose
and then gloriously kicked over and destroyed just before leaving
with shrieks that the barbarian hordes in history would have been
proud of. And there was still the bus trip back and the journey was
so short that I wouldn't feel sick, I really wouldn't, this time.

Mother was happiest in the summer, swimming and boating and
sunbathing every day. Her skin was always sun-and-wind burned and
Brinnin's description of her rustic and sophisticated charm surely
reflects her appearance then. The frail looks of her latter years, when
she lost weight rapidly and walked slowly, could not have been fore-
seen in those years of exuberant energy.

Arguments

The high spirits were soon to be deflated by Margaret Taylor's news
that my father's American mistress was in London and had been
seen in company with Dylan, who had introduced her to his friends
and had spent a weekend in Brighton with her. A 'blue stocking' and
journalist, she was just the type that my father normally shied away
from; for him to fall for someone on his own intellectual level was
not only stimulating but threatening to his marriage. Encouraged, she
followed him to London in the summer of 1950 and was openly introduced to his friends but not, of course, to Caitlin. John Malcolm Brinnin
would later claim that Father told him how he was in love with both
his wife and 'Sarah' (whose real name was Pearl Kazin).

In keeping his encounter with his American mistress secret, he
had not anticipated Margaret's honesty. When denying the charges

of infidelity to the McAlpines, Father referred to Margaret as the 'grey fiend'. With hindsight, my mother thought Margaret's revelations showed how she felt herself involved in the betrayal. By sharing letters with Caitlin she hoped they could act together against this foreign interloper. Mother read the letters in mounting horror and fury.

I can remember the subsequent shouting matches between my parents, which could be heard in the kitchen area. I heard such phrases as 'That American bitch' repeated over and over while Dad denied everything; he claimed that this American woman was a purely professional contact. In fact, they had met over an interview in New York.

'Liar,' countered Mother to anything he said, adding the words which I wasn't to use, 'bastard' and 'fuck you'.

'Oh, she's at him again,' said Dolly who did not know enough to take Mother's side. 'You wait till they've had a few tonight. She'll kill him.'

Later that day, while I waited for Father's return from his shed, I saw Mother getting ready, arranging her hair and makeup at the dressing-table.

'If you see your father, say I'm at the Mariner's,' she said.

I knew the significance of changing their usual pub for another. I tried to stay awake to hear them returning together and when I woke to a loud slam at the front door but no arguing, I felt relief and fell asleep. I woke again to the front door opening more quietly, and concluded that my parents had returned separately. Next morning I saw Father on the sitting-room bed, its Welsh yellow cover on the floor, and I realized this was a proper quarrel. My parents were not speaking to each other, or to us.

'Will you read to me tonight?' I asked hopelessly.

His 'Umphh' meant 'No'.

Later that morning, I watched him slinking in and out of the house with no greetings. At that moment Father reminded me of Mably, slipping round the rocks when he was in disgrace.

After a few days, gradually my parents began to speak to each other again in cold, subdued tones, the atmosphere chilly like the deteriorating weather. Autumn was on its way. Now my parents' quarrel had filtered down to me and I felt the lack of warmth.

'The trouble is, you look so much like your father,' Mother said when I asked for explanations. 'The harder I pull your curls, the better I feel.'

After a Christmas spoilt by the bad 'atmosphere', my father left for Persia to write a film script for a documentary commissioned by the Anglo-Iranian Oil Company (which became British Petroleum). He went with the producer Ralph Keene, known as 'Bunny'. His brief was to extol the positive financial role played by the company in its host country. My father left behind my mother, who was intent on leaving him. Only the practicalities of taking children and luggage down to her mother's and the added inconvenience of my interrupted schooling made her hesitate. We had been in the Boat House for less than two years and the creative idyll was starting to disintegrate. She decided to stay until another escape route could be arranged.

My father knew of Mother's unforgiving mood and wrote frantic letters of eternal love, interwoven with descriptions of the shocking poverty and civilized wealth he encountered in Persia. He interjected humour over descriptions of Bunny's hypochondria and his 'enormous medicine chest': 'The long Bunny is still in bed, groaning: he has a "little chill", he says, has a huge fire in his room, two hot water bottles, an array all over his bedside table of syrups, pills, syringes, laxatives, chlorodyne, liniments and compresses; he uses a thermometer every hour.'

He also wrote of his fears for their marriage: 'Caitlin beloved, unless you write to say that we will be together again, I shall die . . . There will be nothing put pains and nightmares and howlings in my head and endless endless nights and forsaken days until you say, "I am waiting. I love you."' When she did not reply, he reminded her of their love and family life: 'WRITE. I'm lost without you. Tell me about Colm, Aeron and Llewelyn. I'll send Llewelyn stamps of Iran. My dear! Dylan.'

The cold letter he was dreading arrived: 'Caitlin dear, your letter, as it was meant to, made me want to die.' He told her that he planned to fly back on 14 February and stay with the McAlpines in London. Unless she sends a message of reconciliation, he'll know 'everything is over'.

In the meantime, Mother became more attentive towards me than usual. Her coldness had turned to affectionate gestures as if she were drawing the children around her and she had confided that we might go away for a long time, maybe with my cousins, Aunt Brigit and Granny Macnamara in Blashford, Hampshire. She didn't say anything about Dylan not finding us on his return.

As it turned out we were all there at Laugharne as usual when he did. By late February, after an uneasy reconciliation with Mother, he was back home, writing his usual stream of pleading letters.

*

By the same time a year later, in 1951, Mother was pregnant again and determined to terminate the pregnancy. She meant to accompany Dylan on his next American tour 'to fend off the fawning fans and she hyenas.' I heard Mother telling Brigit about the trip she and my father were going to make to the United States. 'The problem is Aeron,' she said. Why was I a problem? I had plenty of friends in Laugharne. Why couldn't I stay at the Boat House, extending largesse (egg and chips, blackberry and apple pie) to all my friends. Dolly would be there to cook and look after Colm and me, surely.

Mother complained to everyone about the 'American vultures' about to descend but only two mild-mannered men, one looking arty but smart in shiny shoes, appeared one day and stayed for the weekend. They were John Malcolm Brinnin, organizer of Dad's visits to America, and his friend Bill Read. The weekend with us was a disaster.

An enormous fight erupted during lunch. Before anyone could eat, my mother and father were fighting, rolling on the floor towards the kitchen where Dolly and I watched. Once it was over Dolly went to clear up the scattered plates and cutlery and food, while my father went to his shed and my mother confided her grievances to the two Americans. The two men could not help but sympathize.

Illness and Summer Visitors

About that time Mother and I caught mumps. I remember Mother looking after me as I lay on the sitting room divan that was usually covered with a bright yellow weave, now thrown on the floor.

When Colm or I were unwell, we were transferred downstairs from our sickbeds to the general living room. Here Mother could chat to Dylan and visitors or speak on the phone while keeping an eye on the patient. I must have been really unwell because the outline of my mother bending over me was hazy and seemed to alternate from clear to indistinct. It was made worse when teams of ants seemed to be trooping across the white wall and descending on to my pale blue blanket and even over Mother. I warned her in a feeble voice but she seemed unworried by them. I felt the sweat prickle on my forehead and threw off my last covering, shivering hot and cold under the sheet. Mother put back one of the blankets with an uncharacteristic gentleness. Normally, she would have thrown it over in one brutal gesture that showed she was worried about me. That, of course, was before she contracted mumps herself and we had to run around fulfilling her needs.

From nowhere a tall figure loomed by the fireplace, with a shock of white hair and a bushy white and grey beard, a black homburg in his hand. He was dressed in black, a bright kerchief at his neck. He appeared not to notice me; and the ants grew more numerous as I fixed my bleary eyes on the visitor. My parents were talking to Augustus John. I could hear my father telling Augustus about me.

'She's really very good,' he said in an echo of Granny's praise. 'Much quieter when she's ill.'

Would Augustus suspect what a noisy pest I could be when people ignored me, I wondered, as Augustus continued to ignore the ants and me. Instead, he sat down on the only comfortable armchair to light a pipe. Whenever he travelled to West Wales, he would visit us. He was staying with Richard Hughes at Castle House and was on his way to reignite friendships with the travelling Romany gypsies assembled near Tenby. In earlier days, he spent long periods immersing himself in Romany lore and culture, painting the dark-eyed, colourfully dressed gypsies vying with their brighter caravans, backdrops of orange, green and yellow.

The same summer, after both Mum and I had recovered from our nasty bouts of illness, my godmother, Elisabeth Lutyens, also came to visit. She was not a pretty woman but had a strong presence, expressive gestures and loud haw-haws of laughter. Mother told her the sad story of the latest quarrel as they sat around drinking beer – not bothering to transfer baccy tin, bottles and glasses to the veranda though the sun was shining. One night, on the way back from the Brown's, my father had threatened suicide after a quarrel with Mother – so loud I'd heard them from the house as they zigzagged down the path. Mother said Dad was 'a low son of a bitch, a liar and a deceiver' and that he had left 'forever'.

'Good riddance to the bastard,' repeated Mother; but you could tell she was worried where he could be.

The phone rang and I put my spoon down from my burnt scrambled egg to hear better. It was Dad phoning from Swansea, she told Elisabeth. Mother came into the kitchen, shouting out to Elisabeth that they'd better have something to eat before collecting 'the blighter'. At this, Colm started to whine and Mother was forced to feed us, too, with meat pie prepared by Dolly the day before. She packed up a bag of clothes, bread and biscuits to tide us over and soon Colm and I were dumped unceremoniously at Dolly's.

I don't remember Elisabeth making a visit for a while after, not encouraged by having to pay the taxi to bring the missing husband home and having to stock up the empty pantry. When they arrived to collect the errant husband, both Mother and Father were crying separately, described by Elisabeth as 'indulging in much snivelling'. My father's shoulders and head were down in a penitent position while Mother was upright and accusing. After half-an-hour they took the drama to another pub, downing drinks regularly, with Elisabeth reminding them they had to get back. They were oblivious to her with Father denying everything and Mother's indignation with his infidelity lessening from pub to pub.

Soon Elisabeth stopped trying to drink as much as them as she was responsible for getting them home. The whole day was taken up with more pub stops to sort out their differences, both revelling in the drama, according to Elisabeth. She said that the basic problem was my father's infidelities which Mother could not accept, not considering her own peccadilloes as comparable to his. She could never hope to even the score as his opportunities were much greater than hers.

Despite the anxiety, my father managed the daily routine of writing. After completing *The Times* cryptic crossword with D.J. in the morning, he was writing 'Do Not Go Gentle Into That Good Night' about his dying, nearly blind father in the afternoon. As he wrote to Princess Caetani, 'The only person I can't show (the enclosed) poem to is, of course, my father, who doesn't know he's dying'. Princess Caetani, an active, handsome American-born princess, lived in Rome where she financed and ran the literary magazine called *Botteghe Oscure*.

So often demanding and negligent towards his employers, by contrast he showed generosity and considerateness to struggling new poets and students, answering their questions in person or by letter. In the summer of 1951, he wrote to the young poet Douglas Phillips commending his explosions of 'cocks and cunts and blood and stars and great green cabbages. I read the poems right through quickly, bits of them aloud and always with excitement, for it is exciting being in at the beginning of a new talent, however mixed-up it may be at the moment.' In a generous gesture, he promises to send two of Phillips's poems to *Botteghe Oscure* and invited him to stay for a weekend.

Another instance of his better side was demonstrated at a recording he made for the BBC immediately after the war in the makeshift Cardiff broadcasting studios. With producer Elwyn Evans in charge, Dylan gave a talk on Welsh connections in poetry, followed by the broadcaster and solicitor John Darran. Outside the broadcast Evans asked Dylan the pronunciation of his name to which he replied: 'Welsh people call me Dullon . . . the English call me Dilun (Dylan). My friends call me Shitface.' Dylan finished his recording at 5.30 p.m. but declined sloping off to the local pub and insisted on staying to hear Darran's contribution. Evans feels that Dylan responded sympathetically to Darran's lame leg and wished to show solidarity. He said, 'I think the bad leg appealed to him.'

All three eventually repaired to the local bar but an unsettling incident soon broke up the camaraderie. A complete stranger came up to my father and accused him of deserting the Welsh language, with the provocative: 'Call yourself a Welshman. Why don't you bloody well write in Welsh, then?' Though he didn't deign to answer the atmosphere was broken and the friendly party went their separate ways.

My father's productivity during the spring and summer of 1951 came to an end when he needed to spend more time in London and had to make arrangements for his forthcoming American tour to begin at the opening of the following year.

Leaving Laugharne

In preparation for the American tour, the entire family, together with Dolly and her son, Desmond, moved to 54 Delancey Street, Camden Town, a basement flat found by Margaret Taylor. She hoped that, by bringing the caravan from Oxford as a 'writing den' in the back garden, this would make Dylan less keen to work abroad. She feared that the American tours were wrecking his health and talent and hoped the BBC might relent and employ him as a full-time broadcaster. She called on her contacts to promote his cause but with little success, as his perceived unreliability was universally accepted, despite not being founded in fact. His habit of frequenting the local pubs around Portland Place and Fitzrovia was shared by most of the BBC staff in those days, being a convenient and pleasant environment to discuss future programmes and projects. Many useful contacts were made by my father in this way.

Mother thought Margaret was keen to house the family in order to keep Father away from the sexual temptations of America. Margaret's feelings for my father were certainly complex and, though she was kind to his family, she was jealously antagonistic to outsiders. She was a loving person and her affection for my father spilt over into admiration and sympathy for Caitlin and affection for me.

Saying goodbye to my friends from Laugharne was terrible. Like me, my father had to leave more than friends. Some of the villagers and the locals in the Brown's had inspired the characters in *Under Milk Wood*, and Laugharne together with its residents would remain in his thoughts. William Watts was an independent draper in the haberdashery shop between the newsagent and butcher along Market Street. He wore a panama hat, butterfly collar, bow-tie and shiny shoes and was always dapper and smart, just as we imagine the radio play's equivalent, Mog Edwards. However, in the Laugharne haberdashery there was no gadgetry for change to 'hum along the wires' (as described in *Under Milk Wood*) which could be found at the upmarket T.P. Hughes store in Carmarthen. William Watts was not engaged like his counterpart to Miss Price of the sweet-shop but was a married man with a silent wife and talkative daughter. Richard Lewis remembers the dapper draper saying of them, 'and as for our Margaret, not a word and as for Gwen she talks like a book'.

The butcher at St Clears, four miles up the road, who looked the part in his striped apron, was called Carl Eynon and reputedly inspired the Butcher Beynon. The butcher was conveniently located near the pub patronized by my father, who was invited occasionally to sample the faggots and cowl prepared in the kitchen behind the shop. Waves of tantalizing aromas would waft to the pub; my father's imagined corgi chops were definitely not part of the menu.

The butcher in Laugharne from whom we usually bought our meat was Ralph Burnham Gleed, who also wore a stripey apron and had a stripey awning over his shop next to the haberdashery run by William Watts. In spite of the credit extended to the Thomas family, his sister Silvia tells me that my mother complained that one steak he sold her was tough enough to tan a shoe. By all accounts, Butcher Beynon was clearly an amalgam of all the butchers my father had known, with perhaps the two most recent ones in Laugharne and St Clears uppermost in his mind when he was writing *Under Milk Wood*.

Other characters lifted from real life cannot be found in *Under Milk Wood* because they were transformed for the purposes of literature. This cannot be said for my father's prose broadcast, 'Laugharne' (recorded on 5 October 1953), just before his final U.S. tour in which Danny Raye is referred to by his real name. It is only a passing, affectionate reference to the well-known Laugharne character who would draw his pension, go on a drinking spree and after pub closing hours sing in the street, with boots or rubbish thrown from residents eager to sleep.

When drunk, he used to walk along the centre line of the road, shouting 'pa-pam', shooting imaginary enemies, entranced by cowboys and Indians like the rest of us. Once he went missing and was found with a gash on his head which required hospital treatment. He played the village fool by participating in the annual carnival, banging an imaginary drum as he marched in front of the band making their way down the hill to the Grist.

Silvia Gleed and her sister Peggy, siblings of butcher Bobby Gleed, remember being entertained by Danny at the St Clears station waiting room, Danny rapping his knuckles on the table there, playing it like a drum. My father used to admire or tolerate Danny doing the same on the pub table, stopping only when the beer bottles jumped up and down.

Danny's son, Donald, one of seven children or more, continues the tradition of providing free foolery for all. Canny, and no fool in reality, he can be found around the Boat House cliffwalk, recalling the days of Dylan and his family in Laugharne. He can remember when his father raised the children on £1 a week in the days that a pint of beer cost 9 pence. Looking like his father did in my own father's day, Danny turns up at the town carnival, one tooth in his head, smiling broadly and dressed like a fisherman in a thick familiar knit, flat cap and wellies. He is proud of winning third place in the pancake race in his wellies when in his seventies.

'With my daps, I'd have won the race,' he claims, pointing to past rugby glory.

Exchanging his flat cap for a knitted hat and enlisting the help of Pearla, his wife, they won first prize as Compo and Nora Batty (from *Last of the Summer Wine*) in the fancy dress competition. 'It was a walkover,' he proudly claims, with Pearla wearing curlers and lisle stockings falling to the ankles.

In my father's broadcast, 'Laugharne', he refers to other Laugharne institutions: the Rolls Royce, the Portreeve (a member of the local council) and other local inhabitants. Fish and chips were sold from the Rolls Royce, adapted with a fryer and probably a gas container by Laugharne local Arthur Jenkins. He parked on the Strand to sell his chips or drove around the town.

Once, Mr Jenkins got into difficulty. Although he should have known better, he was caught in his Rolls by a spring tide. Along it came, lapping at a rate of knots across the flat area of scrub and sea grasses of the Strand and not stopping even for Mr Jenkins and the Rolls, however much he tried to wave it away and reason with the tide. We offered to give a push when the engine was slow in responding, but this was turned down with an impatient, 'Get out of the way, kids,' as if it was our fault. Finally, the large, ponderous car started to move with a shudder away from the incoming water, somewhat to our disappointment, though we were glad to have our fish and chips, exact money held tightly in our palms. For us children, that was the high point of excitement for the day which we would embellish to anyone who was not fortunate enough to see it live, probably adding that we had helped push the car and Mr Jenkins out of danger.

The 'St Bernard (without brandy)' referred to in the 'Laugharne' broadcast was an animal owned by Colonel Wilson of Glan-y-mor, the grand house overlooking the bay, and it was the terror of Laugharne inhabitants. People shinned up trees and bolted their doors when Sam escaped from the extensive grounds where he and the colonel lived. Glan-y-mor was situated above the Boat House and the cliffwalk, which they would often use. They were devoted to one another. When the owner died, the St Bernard lifted the coffin lid and slept there, inconsolable, before the decision was taken to put the dog out of his misery.

The autumnal days were still warm when we set off for London and Camden Town. At the station, Mother, Dolly, Colm, who had just turned three, and I were installed with all our paraphernalia in one carriage by Tudor Williams, while my father immediately disappeared to another. I was not worried as I knew he would be reading his thrillers in blessed peace and munching his way through a brown paper bag of boiled sweets. Tudor Williams, dressed in stout boots, gaiters and warm jacket, stood on the platform of Carmarthen station as if making sure the train would start.

The train was letting out bursts of steam. Dolly looked apprehensive about the journey and the thought of moving somewhere new. She looked as if she might suddenly jump out, dragging Desmond behind her. Desmond himself was quiet as the grave and just as withdrawn. Then the train started to move, the smelly white steam forming banners outside our window, rogue curls creeping into our carriage, the engine gaining speed and the steam shrouding Mr Williams, our last contact with home, from our sight. Dolly burst into tears.

'Come on,' chided Mother not unsympathetically, 'let's open the sandwiches.'

The baskets were brought down from the luggage rack and we ate for Britain; only a few welsh-cakes in grease-proof paper were left. 'You can eat,' Dolly said to me but I was eating extra to cover for Desmond. He sat in a corner, his knees to his chin (ignoring pleas not to put his feet on the seat) and would not eat. 'I've kept some sandwiches for Desmond,' said Dolly, showing us her secret cache. I did not think he would eat them until he returned safely to Laugharne.

When nearly at Paddington, my mother said accusingly to me, 'Where's your father?'

'Oh, he's only in the next compartment but one,' I said knowledgably, having checked on my first lavatory outing.

'He won't be there,' said Mother even more knowledgably. She was judging by previous train journeys. 'Look for him in the buffet-car and tell him to come and help *at once*.'

'Do you mean the buffet?' I asked rhyming buffet with tuffet, like Miss Muffet in the nursery rhyme.

'Oh, go on, silly,' said my mother, echoing my father. In an affectionate mood, he would call me 'Silly Billy', putting his arm round my shoulders if I told a lie, or a truth embroidered beyond recognition, or, as in this case, something I knew was inaccurate. I liked to pretend not to know certain words so they wouldn't know how much I listened and gathered information from the grown-ups.

I made my way down the corridor of the swaying train, negotiating and jumping over the moving floor from one coach to another, better than any funfair. Wisps of white swept past the train windows of the corridor with views of terraced houses starting to appear and occasional scrappy green spaces, with no sheep, bordering the rail.

My father was parked on a bar stool, a glass of beer on the counter and beer tumbler circles near his glass, talking to the barman. A standing travel companion with glass in hand interjected comments and shook his head in agreement. From his increased height, my father looked down at me with increasing recognition but with no word of greeting.

'Mother says you've got to come and help,' I stated, my mission accomplished. 'We'll be getting to Paddington soon.'

'Yes,' agreed the barman, '23 minutes if we're on time.'

'Keeps pretty good time all considered,' said the stranger who wanted to be part of the conversation. 'Except for now and then. I travel regular business in town,' he said, making his presence felt.

'I've seen you before,' said the barman, expansively including even the travelling salesman, an obvious interloper.

The barman and my father returned to their own conversation, as a stale bath bun was slipped to me ('They'll only be thrown away') from under a dome-shaped cover. I kept the bun for Desmond, nibbling a little of the side with the most currants just to test what it was like. The tea urn hissed its disapproval.

As the train drew up in Paddington, I told my father he'd cop it now. He quickly finished the beer he had just ordered and fussed us off the train, having difficulty with the door catch. On the platform my mother and Dolly looked like refugees carrying Colm, luggage and baskets. I expected my mother to deliver a tirade. But when she saw us she smiled and gathered us to the family group like stray sheep. I was constantly amazed by her fluctuating temper; sometimes for no apparent reason she would suddenly attack my father with bitter accusations and punches thrown at his shoulders or his head. At other times, he seemed to escape her anger when he most deserved it. I was glad there was to be no row on the platform with Dolly and Desmond in tow. They were looking around in wide-eyed, terrified wonder at the trains, the huge arc of the station roof with its steel girders, and the surging mass of humanity intent on its own business.

Somehow six of us arrived at 54 Delancey Street. I looked around our new home and found it strangely comforting that the walls were covered with a large floral pattern chosen by Margaret Taylor from the same ream that covered the walls in Oxford. I could lie in bed or muse in the day, following the intricate patterning and repetition of the design.

Quickly the same routine we had adopted in Laugharne was recreated here. Dolly cooked when my parents were visiting the local pub by the railway sidings. When they returned Mother wanted to heat a stew or fry an egg and sausage or once, ambitiously, make tripe and onions stewed in milk. We would also go walking on Primrose Hill or on scraps of green left over by the grudging lines of roads and houses and shops. It was strange to live without the sea and fields around us but my nomadic life had fitted me for changes and I soon adapted. As part of the routine, my father would retire in the afternoon to his caravan in the garden to write until opening time.

On Saturday nights my father and mother invited friends to our local or went to the Ravenscourt Arms in Hammersmith, opposite the house belonging to Cordelia and Harry Locke. The artist Ruskin Spear, a friend who rented a studio at the top of the house, sometimes joined them, though he favoured the Carpenters Arms nearby. Barbara and Bob Sloane, who worked in the car rental and airline business, were part of the same set.

Desmond and I started to attend Primrose Hill School and in spite of my Welsh accent soon fitted in, enjoying the work and play. It was here that I first fell for poetry, encouraged by a male teacher who read out 'The Song of Hiawatha' with a powerful voice and a masterful understanding of the trance-like rhythm. I could hear what Longfellow must have intended through the performance. I hoped he would go on forever with his Tum te Tum te Tum te Tum te:

Downward through the evening twilight,
In the days that are forgotten,
In the unremembered ages.
From the full moon fell Nokomis,
Fell the beautiful Nokomis,
She a wife, but not a mother.

'Dad, do you write poems like Hiawatha?' I asked.
'Not as good as that,' he said, and quoted lines from the work.

Work at school was very different as well. Exams were not even talked about. At Laugharne Infants School there was constant talk of the 11-plus and the entrance to the grammar school in Carmarthen, which gave a competitive edge to all our studies. Although one of the students most favoured in the 11-plus stakes (eventually winning a place at Carmarthen), I hated to see the faces of my companions fall whenever preparatory tests were announced and they anticipated failure.

Desmond was younger than me and in another class so when he started to refuse to go to school, making us late, I was annoyed with him. When, at weekends, he was found standing in a corner on one leg, I realized that all was not well and in the end Desmond and Dolly had to be sent back to Laugharne earlier than anticipated. Probably Desmond, the shyest of boys, could not adapt to the change. In Laugharne we all respected his silences and allowed him the time he seemed to need to ponder and weigh-up all suggestions made to him. After what seemed to an impatient child an eternity, he would turn away mumbling that he had better be going to the kitchen and Dolly, 'cos Booda's there and has some comics for me' or 'Llewelyn's due on the train'.

One of the last times I saw Desmond was years later, outside the Brown's Hotel in the main street, clad in motorbike leathers and looking like a mini John Travolta, surrounded by teenagers. Girls looked up at him adoringly, a dark brilliantined curl falling over his arching brow. Even I, a very immature teenager, recognized he was smouldering with sex appeal. In the crowd was a mini-skirted slip of a girl with blue eyes and dark, wavy hair, just recognizable as Shelagh, with her own group of admirers. Obviously, both Desmond and

Shelagh were happiest at home amongst people they knew. A few years on, Dolly took me to visit Desmond with his family of four or five children and his wife as nervy and slim as a teenager. He looked resigned and even happy with his brood.

The Old Haunts

As winter approached, my father continued broadcasting and writing. He also found time to visit his old haunts in Soho and Fitzrovia, both areas within reach of Broadcasting House. One of his favourite pubs had always been the Fitzroy Tavern on the corner of Windmill Street and Charlotte Street.

When Dolly had to leave with Desmond, Mother was left to look after two children, which she did in her usual haphazard, cheerful way. In fact, she seemed happier than I had seen her lately in the Boat House. Every evening, she left me to fend with Colm and met up with friends on the pub rounds. I did not mind as Colm went to sleep at 7 p.m. exactly and rarely woke before 7 a.m. He seemed to trust me implicitly, not realizing I was only a child myself. When he did wake up because the bedclothes had fallen off or he wanted a drink, I would cuddle him before putting him back to sleep. We had an understanding that I wasn't going to share with Mother.

She, meantime, would stay out till all hours, often at weekends taking bottles back to a friend's flat or basement. While in London, my father introduced her to the regulars at the Fitzroy. She already knew Nina Hamnett, a painter and illustrator originally from Tenby, and everyone seemed to know J.M. Tambimuttu, publisher and literary facilitator. He recommended Dylan to editors of literary journals when he first visited London and was not well known. Mother's dress for the evening became more colourful, with satins and silk, organdie and a flowing purple cloak to keep off the winter chill. However, she had competition at the Fitzroy, which she recounted to a friend in Laugharne; a colourful racing tipster Prince Monolulu, alias Peter McKay, who often wore full Kenyan national costume.

The Fitzroy was an old stamping ground for Mother and it was nearby at the Wheatsheaf that Augustus John first introduced her to my father in 1936. Augustus knew everyone, she said: Wyndham Lewis, Walter Sickert and Jacob Epstein as well as many notables from Portland Place including radio presenters, poets and performers. Other characters she remembered were Charlie Drake, whom she found just as amusing as Dylan, Gilbert Harding and Beverley Nichols, not forgetting Norman Wisdom. She told me she and Dylan got on instantly, with Dylan proposing on his knees after an hour's acquaintance, soon chalking up a bill to Augustus's name while at his hotel, possibly taking advantage of Mother's status as Augustus's sometime mistress.

The Swiss Tavern (known by some as the Helvetia) in Old Compton Street was also a popular venue for artists, including my father. This was where he was to accidentally leave his original manuscript of *Under Milk Wood* just before his last tour to the States in 1953. Mother was particularly incensed by the entire incident. Douglas Cleverdon, the radio producer, delivered duplicate copies of *Under Milk Wood* to my father at the air terminal, much to his relief. He asked Cleverdon to look for the original manuscript while he was away in America and he found it behind the bar of the Swiss Tavern. After my father's death a few weeks later, he claimed that it was his – Dylan had told him to keep it, he said. He then went on to sell it to the Times Book Co. Ltd., which in turn sold it on again.

When Mother disputed this story and laid claim to the manuscript, taking Cleverdon to court in 1966, she discovered that she had two other institutions to fight in order to reclaim it. She was convinced that one of her star witnesses, Daniel Jones, gave the wrong impression in court, turning up like a Hollywood extra for bohemian living in a bright velvet jacket and kerchief which in those days spelt unreliability in the face of the Establishment, especially when compared to the successful radio producer and the two prestigious institutions who were the recipients of the manuscript after him. She lost the case and at least £13,000, a huge sum for those days.

The revisiting of friends did not always take place in the neutral, preferred milieu of the pub. I accompanied my father on one of his visits to the Irish poet Louis MacNeice and his wife Hedli Anderson.

'There are children for you to talk to,' he reassured me.

'But how do I know I'll like them?' I queried. Or them me, I thought.

I found myself in the kitchen with two or three children of around my age, shooting a desperate glance at my father's retreating back as he disappeared with Louis. Hedli, an opera singer, could be heard practising, her voice seeping through the crack of the sitting-room door, along the skirting of the entrance hall and under the kitchen door. As she hit the high notes, the glasses shuddered.

When she eventually appeared, a fiery presence with red hair, I saw that such a strong voice had found a natural home. She was so overwhelming, though all she did was fill a glass with water, I stopped speaking to observe her. After a while, Dad reappeared with a glass of beer in one hand, a book in another, with a kindly warning that I had to stop enjoying myself as it was time to go. He had caught the MacNeice children and me laughing loudly. The children seemed intrigued by my life at Laugharne. I interpreted their smiles of amusement as proof of my narrative skills. I suppose they could have been laughing at me but it did not seem so. More than once they had to ask me to repeat words because of my strong Welsh accent. One of them was a red-headed teenager about to blossom into her mother. I was both glad and disappointed to leave.

Louis and Dad stood at the door, Louis towering but unassuming as if he were the short one. He helped my father with his coat while Hedli fussed with mine. I took it from her and slipped my arms into the sleeves, smiling to show I appreciated the help. Hedli and Louis were both so much taller and bigger than the people I knew, except Augustus. It was like living in *Gulliver's Travels* and finding that the inhabitants of Brobdingnag (tall as church spires) behaved in much the same way as the Lilliputians and took no advantage of their height.

We also visited my aunt, Nicolette Devas, at 12 Carlyle Square. Laurie Lee, who later wrote *Cider with Rosie*, was sometimes there without Kathy, his new wife. He was always warm and friendly towards everyone, including me. He had lived in the top room at Markham Square, writing and playing his violin. On one of my visits, when we found Laurie chatting to Nicolette in the basement kitchen, I fell down the stairs on to my head. He rushed out to help me, held my forehead as I vomited green bile, and dabbed my brow with a kitchen cloth from the sink. He waited until the shock of the moment passed, his arm around my shoulders, in perfect sympathy. Another time at a drinks party, still a child, I sprang an unexpected toothache which he and another charismatic friend jointly told me would disappear the moment one of them touched my cheek. True to their word, the splitting toothache departed at the touch of fingers . . . I was most grateful.

At a gathering much later, at Limerston Street off King's Road where Nicolette was living with her second husband, Rupert Shephard, Laurie told me that he definitely preferred small women. I glowed. He had the ability to find merit where others might find only deficiencies. He told me about *Cider with Rosie* and how Nicolette was the first to encourage a book about Slad and his boyhood reminiscences, which he completed over four years while lodging with the Devases in his Markham Square attic, playing the violin in breaks. It took him a year of intensive work to complete the book and a further one to cut the material by two-thirds.

After four months in London, my parents left for New York for a lecture tour in January 1952, which was to last for another four months. It was a shock when Margaret came to collect me. Someone had forgotten to tell me. She could tell I was confused and upset and reassured me that I'd be going to the same school while Mum and Dad were away and that her two girls, Sofia and Amelia, were excited by my arrival. I wondered whether she was just saying this so that I didn't make the usual sobbing and crying accompaniment as the tears coursed down my face unbidden. My mother looked surprised.

'I thought you liked being with them all,' she said, claiming there had been other offers to take me.

I doubted that, as my reputation of being difficult and loud preceded me, although with age I behaved much better, or so Mother's friends said when I was listening without appearing to do so.

The Camden Town interlude had been a failure. Though Mother found the relatively glamorous town life an improvement on 'the bogs of Laugharne', my father's hopes of more BBC work were dashed, perhaps because of his imminent departure. In addition, Margaret was humiliated by hearing my mother and father making derogatory remarks about her. They were standing at the local bar, waiting and unaware that she was already there, eavesdropping without intent, tears pouring down her face. Decades later, Mother told me with a blush how shocked they felt.

'It was just unfortunate she overheard. We were always poking fun at her green cat stews, funny outfits (she tried to copy my style and failed) and her "Duckies . . . isn't this fun . . ." but really we were quite fond of her. She was so good to us.' Margaret's stews were made with peas (the supposed colour of green cat's pee) while Mother's, though more ordinarily brown, had bone marrow fat floating on the surface. She had no right to criticize anyone else's stew.

I knew nothing of this at the time and soon settled happily enough into life at 26 Park Village East, Camden Town, the Taylors' London address after moving from Oxford. The house was large enough for lodgers so there was a succession of young men who appeared at the door or lurked in the hall or the stairway. I learned to ignore them and lived my separate existence with the girls, mainly on the ground floor. I continued at the same school and on my ninth birthday invited classmates to a party. We all giggled so much we were sick and when the Taylor boys, the hugely mature and exciting Sebastian and Giles, came home, they saw our party in chaos.

The boys were a welcome part of the household and teased us unmercifully, scrubbing our backs in the bath and emptying the water before we were ready to get out. Whenever Sebastian or Giles were around, I was not bothered by what they did. They were usually kind and helpful; it was enough that they, gods from Olympus, took some notice of us, three girls under ten.

Florence, the live-in help, and her son, who had grown into an enormous boy, were still part of the Taylor family. She had produced another baby since my last stay, and at first I thought it was the same one who had never grown up. He looked more African than English, a prize-fighter in the making and it was surprising to discover what a sweet nature he possessed, always forgetting any meanness towards him. I fail to understand why we were such wily tormentors.

There was one incident which was particularly nasty. When we were asked to take him with us to the Saturday matinee at the local cinema, we all left the house together, conveniently losing him in the long queues of screaming children outside the doors. We failed to 'see' him afterwards, a bullish though lonely figure looking around for us. We ducked and dived behind the large columns of the cinema and then kept our heads below the hedges of moth-eaten skeletal greenery, avoiding travelling home with him. There, he was in floods of tears, snivelling and wiping his nose on his tight-fitting coat sleeve, Margaret and his mother fussing around him. 'Oh, but we looked everywhere for him,' we said, mealy-mouthed and unrepentant. The cruelty seemed part of the fun of staying with the Taylors.

Mum and Dad Away

Dylan and Caitlin in New York. (Photo courtesy of Reg Evans).

Meantime, my parents were in America with a very different programme. There was far too much travelling, my mother told me. There was ten days' holiday at the beginning, for my mother's sake, and another ten days half-way through the tour. Mother found the rest of the time hard to fill. She spent most of her time shopping at Macy's, her clothes eventually filling what seemed like forty borrowed suitcases and bags. On returning to Laugharne, they filled the bedroom and Mother wailed she had no occasions to wear the clothes she'd bought, particularly two bathing costumes of silver and gold lamé.

She told me later that because she was bored, with not enough to do, she started a diary but soon gave it up. Rollie McKenna, the photographer, took pictures of Mother and Father, Mother not objecting as it was someone she already knew from Laugharne. She felt less relaxed at one of the academic dinner parties, rudely asking, 'Are they all stuffed shirts like you?' Even the constant stream of parties where she despairingly danced solo soon palled. Rose, Brinnin's mother, thought Mother's situation as wife of the celebrity untenable for anyone so spirited.

The rows with my father were becoming legendary. Mother remembered one where green toothpaste was smeared all over a hotel room but could not remember the cause of the row.

It seemed that they thought of us children only when they received urgent messages. In California, where they were staying with their good friend Ruth Witt-Diamant, a professor at San Francisco State University, they were told of Llewelyn's unpaid school fees. Eventually, after a 'colossal row' (Dad had said they were already paid), these were settled via the literary agent David Higham. I am surprised even today that my mother could leave Colm for so long. She was correct in believing that my father, if left alone, would find other women to care for him. He admitted drunkenly in the last few days of his life that all women were 'substitutes' for Caitlin.

They did not completely forget me. My father wrote to Margaret '. . . and how is dear Aeron?' Nevertheless, they did not send me a postcard or letter during their long absence. This did not worry me one jot at the time as I never presumed they would write to me direct. In fact, I never presumed they were going to collect me from Margaret's. I hoped that one day my parents would reclaim me but these hopes could be dashed. The alternative, staying with the Taylors, was not an entirely bleak prospect and with time I'd forget Mum and Dad.

At last my parents came back in the May of 1952, laden with children's books and huge cellophane bags of indecently bright-coloured sweets. Dad and I wanted to go home to Wales straight away; Mother wanted to stay in London.

We stayed for a short time in Nicolette and Anthony Devas' Carlyle Square basement, in spite of Anthony swearing that no Thomas would ever stay in his house after the last time. The Thomases were disturbing house guests. While my father went to the pub or to work, Mother argued with Nicolette. She always knew everyone's Achilles' heel and reduced her sister to self-disgust and tears. When we all moved into the basement, emergency measures were taken and Anthony's sister, Rosie, and son-in-law, Harry Shaw, were asked to take over the flat (leaving their cramped bedsit in Paddington) 'to keep the Thomases out'.

Return to Laugharne

After a two-week delay in London, we returned to Laugharne. In the aftermath of the United States tour, things slowly returned to the monotonous routine so loved by children and artists. Life was touched for me with the glow my father still saw around Mother. She was against him returning to America, admitting his readings were 'good and effective', but noting what they cost him. She could hear the strain in his voice and observe his exhaustion. She complained

Colm, Aeron and Caitlin at the front door of the Boat House.
(Photo courtesy of Tony Vilela).

that no one had shown her round New York – round Harlem and Chinatown – forgetting that Brinnin had arranged a sightseeing day when both of them were bored by the 'sights'.

Slowly, real work started again. *Under Milk Wood*, 'Adventures in the Skin Trade' and 'Prologue' had to compete for time with radio talks and other public engagements which were hardly ever turned down, meaning that Dad had a few days away usually in Cardiff or London.

I continued with Mother to keep Dad's writing shed tidy. Through the uncurtained windows we could see hills in the distance, green and lush at this time of year. Letters from famous people were binned by Dad if they were not immediately useful. 'I was not much better,' admitted Mother, 'and if it wasn't his work, would "tidy" it away.' There were boxes of papers on the floor of the hut – a fire hazard with the anthracite stove. I enjoyed 'helping' and would draw on the letters and papers about to be 'cleared'. As my father became aware that any scrap of paper could bring in dollars he would save his worksheets (often with bills to tradesmen listed on the same pages) to send to the anthologist Oscar Williams or other American acquaintances.

Virtually nothing was brought back from the gruelling American tour. It had been an expensive time staying in hotels, buying drinks in pubs and Mother purchasing so many clothes. 'I went a bit mad,' she later said, 'I had never seen such abundance.' Very little money was brought home after the extra stop in London either. The usual desperate letters were sent to the usual recipients. Happily unaware of money worries and used to rows, I lived in a world unmarked by trouble.

We returned to Laugharne at the end of May or the beginning of June in 1952, which heralded the imminent arrival of our better-weather visitors. By the summer, when visitors were at their height, we invited and pressed them to be an audience for our plays in the ugly boat shed on the kitchen level. One or two of the stronger visitors could usually be persuaded to carry Granny down to join us. The boat shed was built of dark weather-beaten wooden planks, creosoted a dark brown colour but overlaid by the green tidemark of autumn and spring tides. For some reason the floor was built on two levels, the higher level descending to a lower one so that the stage area was nearer the house. This meant that the non-paying customers had to enter the theatre either by the side entrance, walking over slippery grass, mud and loose stones, or bypass it by crossing the stage to the auditorium.

We took our plays very seriously. Mother was our favourite director for musicals and pantomimes because she interwove the dance and songs so well, though her complicated routines had to be controlled. We insisted that she wrote solo dance numbers wherever possible to allow for improvisation. Cliff Gordon, a professional actor (who played Willy Nilly in the London production of *Under Milk Wood*) wrote one of our plays but he sacrificed the music and dance for words. The play was 'The Smugglers and Exciseman', inspired by the Boat House's history of smuggling.

Mother complained that we were not serious enough when one of the actors skived off to collect comics from Booda, to greet visitors or to fortify ourselves with some of Dolly's apple tart. One of the resident hairdressers in Laugharne, Leonora John, known as Lennie, remembers Mother lending her a pair of red tap shoes and draping us with shawls and flounces from her wardrobe. I can remember a straw boater that Mother used for her Carmarthen market visits being decorated with flowers from the garden.

That summer, the audience for our panto – at least 20 – included Nicolette and Anthony Devas and children, Geraldine Lawrence from Tenby and perhaps Laurie Lee. The play was loosely based on 'Cinderella' and was delayed by my father, who was late for lunch. I found him in the Brown's bar at the table in the bay window, where he normally sat with Mother in the evening, playing Nap and Chase the Ace. He was perusing the crossword, with a pint of beer, shared his card winnings with me (ten boiled sweets and two ha'pennies), and agreed to leave for the play. He said that Ivy had given him some stew and he had forgotten his promise to attend.

'What should I buy?' I asked him. 'A liquorice bootlace or one of those red coloured lollipops . . . you know . . . with the white stripes?' I always found it difficult to decide when faced with choices.

'Um,' he deliberated as if he'd been asked a vital question. 'I'd say a chocolate mouse.'

'I haven't enough money,' I objected.

He put his hand in his pocket, jangling change, but we were nearly home.

'I'll ask Mum,' I said, to hurry him along.

Father clapped as loud as the others and kept awake for the show. He had once fallen asleep and was woken by Mother who was furious with him, interrupting the play to shout at him, though he was sacrificing an hour's work for our art.

Life in Laugharne continued after the exodus of the heady summer visitors of 1952. Once in the middle of the night, I was wakened from deep sleep by swearing below my bedroom window. When I looked out I could see that David (barely out of his teens) was helping his father, Cross House landlord Phil Richards, and my father down the slope to the front door. He had to avoid my father's broken arm, in a black sling. The older men managed to stay upright until Father tripped on the steps.

'Are you all right?' I heard David ask.

'Of course . . . I'm always doing this,' answered my father.

Mother came downstairs, mumbling to herself, but unconcerned, 'Bloody man . . .'

They all stayed up for a nightcap and eventually my parents stumbled up the narrow staircase. In the morning everything was back to normal.

My father and Phil Richards were Laugharne allies in after-hours drinking and pig sharing, which Phil kept in the yard beside the Cross House. In the year he would fatten it up and a specialist butcher would visit Laugharne in the spring to slaughter all the pigs. Dad had a share in the pig which provided hocks and bacon for months to come. In addition, Phil would run him round in a natty 1934 10 Standard car in any outings they arranged. In the bar, my father rarely sat down but liked to talk standing up, smoking Jet and Ace cigarettes. When inspired, he would dig around his pocket for a pencil stub or his fountain pen to make notes on the back of his cigarette packets.

One day, I heard my father running down the stairs – usually he walked carefully – and burst into the kitchen with a letter in his hand. He was panting from the unaccustomed exertion and blurted out the news that he had won the Foyle's Poetry Prize.

'And here's the cheque to prove it . . . two hundred and fifty pounds,' he said waving a piece of paper in the air.

'Let me see it,' said Mother snatching cheque and letter. 'And stop blocking the bloody doorway,' she said either to me or Father.

I wasn't going anywhere as I was enjoying the drama. Unfortunately, my mother discarded her pinny in the kitchen, poured two glasses of beer and disappeared into the dining room. After five minutes, I put my face round the door and was told to go away, so hovered at the other side of the door to hear the excited low murmur of conspirators. I recall another poetry prize, the Etna-Taormina International

Prize, which generated nearly as much excitement. Father was co-winner with the Sicilian writer Salvatore Quasimodo.

The publication of *Collected Poems* in November, with the dedication to Caitlin, was another reason to celebrate, particularly as it received good reviews by Cyril Connolly and Philip Toynbee. His favourite review was by Stephen Spender whom he wrote to thank for his 'understanding' of the poems. Stephen and Natasha Spender were friends whom he had met at Holywell Ford before the war. A previous letter written to Spender was a thinly disguised begging letter.

In spite of the literary success, it was a sad winter. The worst of all was Grandpa's death. On 16 December, at the age of 76, D.J. died from painful throat cancer. Granny always encouraged men to smoke in her presence, providing cut-glass ashtrays, as she thought the practice 'manly'. When Grandpa died, Granny seemed to take his death very well. In his life, my grandfather liked to be known as Jack to differentiate him from the thousands of David Johns in Wales. I read somewhere that my father found the cremation distressing, particularly when someone told him that D.J.'s skull exploded in the furnace, at which point my father vomited. We had many hints that Dad, unlike his mother, was devastated by his father's death. Mother said that he'd always written poetry not only to please himself but his father.

Mother and I found Ivy on the road one day, away from her Brown's Hotel.

'I left Ebi at the bar,' she said. 'It's not the same with Mr Thomas Senior gone.' Mother wanted to know more. 'Dylan's depressed and has no one to do the crossword with now. He doesn't even come for a chat while I'm cooking in the back.'

Mother agreed he was taking his father's death badly.

'With his father gone, he sends his handwritten drafts to Vernon Watkins in Swansea.' She said to Ivy, who seemed a little lost. 'The poems he's working on,' she explained, 'they don't come out of thin air . . . he needs to show them to someone.'

'There's no one at the bar intelligent like the Mr Thomases able to do *The Times* crossword,' said Ivy, returning to her first observation. 'I expect he'll pick up soon,' she said, not sounding too hopeful.

The next hint of Dad's shock and sadness at his father's death was everyone's solicitous enquiries about him. We went to the Cross House for a lemonade after our walk and Phil's wife, who never appeared ordinarily, enquired in grave tones how Mr Thomas was bearing up. Mother answered them all with 'not good', which conveyed to me more than anything else how the death had affected him.

Mother was supportive to my father with the bereavement but was cool about illness. That winter Dolly's mother was unwell and when Dolly would say, 'My mother's under the doctor,' my mother mocked, '. . . Under the *doctor*,' in her imitation of Dame Edith Evans' Lady Bracknell. When I visited Dolly's mother, she said that she was missing her work at the cockle factory, with only her aches and pains to think of and wanted to go back, whatever Dolly or the doctor said. On that occasion, Dolly's mother got out of bed, put on another bed jacket and a coat, and came down the perilous stairs. We ate pickled onions from a jar on the oil tablecloth, part of the cockle factory output. This seemed to exhaust her, so Dolly tucked her up on the sofa in the best room until she had the strength to tackle the stairs again.

These deaths and illnesses hardly touched my own life, which went on its way. Grandpa had withdrawn from me for a long time, only occasionally talking to me or visibly noticing that I was there, talking to Granny at the Pelican, so his physical absence did not affect me. Granny behaved as she had always done. In my world, things couldn't have been better. Dad began reading to me again, despite the undeniable fact that I didn't need reading to at my age – already nine and able to read for myself. It all came about with a book he and Mum gave me at Christmas: a hardback Arthur Rackham-illustrated *The Wind in the Willows* by Kenneth Grahame. Dad had recounted the stories to me by memory so Toady and Mole were old friends.

After recovering from the shock that this was the only present from my parents due to its expense and glossy colour plates, I eventually adopted the stranger into my growing library. I had to put aside my disappointment of the missing stocking with the coal, the pencils and tangerine. The boxes of chocolates which the Carmarthen dentist now forbade – 'too many fillings for someone your age' – were not there either and the boring clothes from Granny took their place. The Grey Lady from Carmarthen, Granny's friend, had sent me some home-knitted bedsocks large enough for a mammoth. I gritted my teeth and they all knew how I felt.

The reading sessions made up for the unpromising, rather adult text I had glanced at with its long sentences and not so easy words, as well as rather a lot of description. I already knew what river banks looked like as I had the Cherwell to draw on.

Dad reading to me was better than ever and I didn't have to rely on him having a bath first. He'd come back extra early to read the next chapter with plenty of breaks for discussion. I'd prepare the decks beforehand: a tumbler of lemonade or Tizer and a bag of hard-boiled sweets or Dolly Mixtures (if Mum gave them from her own supply) placed on a table by his comfy reading chair.

Our talks after the chapter had been read, with Dad modulating his voice differently for each character, centred on our current favourites, the weasels and Toad. After I had pointed out critically that his voice for Toad, hysterical and high as it should be, occasionally slipped into a lower tone, we thought about who was the naughtiest. Was it Toad with his reckless speeding along water, road and airway, ignoring the consequences and not listening to Good Advice from his river cronies? Was it the weasels, ably abetted by the stoats and ferrets happily wrecking Toad Hall when Toad was absent, rightfully imprisoned for his antics? Dad rather favoured Toad with his reckless but amusing ways and said the weasels and their criminal band, carrying guns and other arms as they stood guard, were worse but I knew who was the naughtiest by far.

I argued it out with Dad, pointing out that he didn't like me freewheeling like Toad outside his shed and down the slope of the cliffwalk, especially when I fell and screamed so loud he had to check what was going on, leaving his work and papers.

'The trouble is,' I argued, 'when Toad insisted on taking his friends Moley and Ratty along with him on the road, he made them do everything.'

'Give me an instance,' said Dad, enjoying the debate.

'Well, I was thinking of Toady taking the brightly painted caravan on a holiday and his friends having to look after the horse, watering and feeding it when they stopped, and Toady just sitting wasting time and not helping, just saying how much he loved the open road.'

'You mean he was badly behaved because he involved other people or these two characters in the book?'

'Yes,' I said, thinking I could not have put it better myself.

'But they chose to go because they were worried about Toad getting into trouble,' Dad argued for the defence.

We then discussed the demerits of the weasels, the nasty gang trashing Toad's house while he was away.

'At least Toad had good, loyal friends,' said Dad, 'and he was always so pleased to see them and generous with his hospitality.'

'Are you saying the weasels' only friends were criminals and bad guys because they were nasty themselves?' I said, at least understanding my fathers' argument.

By the New Year there was talk of my parents going to the United States again. Dad had met Brinnin in London and they discussed a new tour, with readings from *Under Milk Wood.*

Throughout the colder months, Mother and I went walking as usual, sometimes in the rain, or so I was told, though my recollections include no showers, squalls or storms. Mother complained about the quagmire of the fields. In long home-knitted shawls, coats scuffed at the cuffs, itchy wool collars, hoods or balaclavas over our eyes, we braved the sandy tidal flats at low tide.

One day we approached Sir John's Hill, the flat, sea-facing side of the Grist where the cocklers' donkeys once grazed. There we found another sheep's carcass, stripped of all flesh, just bones. We usually only found a head or half a set of ribs so a whole skeleton was very exciting. I had been looking for such a treasure for some time.

'Dad, you must see it. It's like a dinosaur in a museum, only smaller. It's all bones and . . .' I struggled to make it exciting. 'And the rib cage is like a cave you can hide in and Mum wants us to draw it or take a picture and you'd better come quick before the tide takes it away.'

He picked his way like a ballet dancer on points across the mud, grass and shingle to our find.

'Can I take a rib for Llewelyn's sea collection?' I begged. 'Can I take a snap with the Brownie?'

'So your mum saw it first?' he asked.

'No, together. We saw it together.' He smiled. 'At the same time.' I didn't mind sharing the glory but wasn't ready to hand it all over to Mum.

'Did Mum do this?' he said placing his muddy foot on the animal's side in the manner of a big game hunter.

I couldn't help laughing. Changing tack, I said: 'Perhaps I could get a shot of Sir John's Hill in the background.'

'Why not just include the fishing boat moored behind it.' Dad was so clever, I thought, and snapped away using up the reel.

'You don't get many this side,' he said, referring to the estuary. It was true. He'd seen many on the Llanstephan and Llanybri side where they grazed but hardly any our side.

With the thought of the next United States tour in April, my father practised his Yeats and Hardy, Roethke and Watkins all through the house, but mostly in what was still the new bathroom, where his voice resonated satisfactorily. Mother would wear a face of gloom which he tried to dispel with promises of holidays in Italy or Portugal and 'no children'. As she was pulling my hair at the time this promise might have sounded attractive, though she still looked glum and disbelieving.

When he talked of work in California with Stravinsky or a post at a university where he would take us all (except Llewelyn, who had to stay in school) she looked as if this might be a possibility. Relenting, she released my head and went to hear Dylan reading and help him choose his programme.

Murder

One day our gentle routine was broken. Dolly was cleaning shoes on pieces of newspaper spread on the veranda; she was smearing on polish with cut-up pieces of vest and seemed to be mumbling, 'He's gone and done it now.' I looked at the shoes lined up like soldiers, two tins of opened Kiwi shoe polish, and a biscuit tin of shoe brushes and rags covered in dried polish. She attacked some mud-covered boots with a kitchen knife.

Mother looked over the balcony, calling Dolly to fetch Booda. Dad had brought the news that the coal sacks had been delivered and were blocking his shed door.

'No thank you,' said Dolly to me. 'I'm not going to get Booda and don't you go to his house neither. It's him that's done it,' she explained.

'What's Booda done'?

'He's only gone and murdered someone,' she said triumphantly.

Running down the path to the Ferry House, I leapt and skipped over the ruts and dips, pretending to be a prize Arab horse whinnying and snorting until I turned the corner of the house on the shore. The Ferry House was built for the elements, a thick-walled white box with tiny windows. Before clambering up to the dirty uncurtained window, I had a drink from the delicious spring which ran down the cliff into my cupped hands. My horse was very thirsty and whinnied gratefully. At the small window I waved my arms about and after a fruitless minute or two had the satisfaction of seeing Booda framed in the door, a dark figure against a deeper well of darkness, the smoke-blackened walls behind. I felt afraid until I gestured my mission and he nodded his understanding, pulling his Dai cap on more firmly and fetching his jacket. He made the shapes of the sacks and mimed counting, but I couldn't tell him how many and shrugged. He followed me up the path but I was only Aeron and Booda couldn't be a murderer. He went to lug the sacks to the Boat House and I returned to Dolly, who said Booda had murdered an old lady the other side of town for her money and everyone knew.

'Will he murder us next?' I asked my mother.

My father seemed only half-interested, staring through the sitting-room window.

'No,' said Mother firmly, 'we haven't any money lying about, and when we do, we give him work. It would be like killing the golden goose.'

'Ah, hah, caught her in a cliché,' I thought inconsequentially but with no time to point it out with all the excitement.

Father seemed unsettled by the coal sacks at his shed door and uncertain how to pass the time. He was used to seeing the view and working on his poems. Finally, he went to the bookshelf in the sitting room and selected a forbidden thriller.

Dolly said she and Booda were waiting to be paid and I hoped Booda would not become impatient waiting. I did not try to talk to my father.

Booda knocked on the door, his clothes more coaly dark than usual and let us know the shed door was accessible. I translated. A coal sack waited by the fuchsia tree to be carried downstairs. Mother always checked what he said with me, his gestures accompanied by uncontrolled moans to emphasise meaning.

I wanted to run up the path with him but went back to Dolly and promised to accompany her home along the cliffwalk as she was more frightened than I was. As we looked over the cliff wall, at the sun dipping behind Sir John's Hill, the shadows were lengthening. You could see the thin coil of grey smoke from the Ferry House, once home to three of Booda's uncles, as he fried his dinner in a pan greasy from countless other dinners.

Scotland Yard moved in the next week. Murders were not frequent and local bobbies not often required to fry such large fish. Mother had talked about golden eggs and I was matching eggs with 'other fish to fry' in various combinations. 'Can't play with you today,' I tried out, 'I've golden eggs and other fish to fry for dinner tonight.' That didn't make sense. I was dangling my legs over the wall, watching the police proceedings. A policeman lifted a fringe of seaweed growing on the lower reaches of rock. Slimy creatures scuttled out and he winced. 'Londoner!' I thought.

'You're not from these parts, then?' I enquired mischievously of the policeman standing in his wellies, head bent while he raked through the mud. He jumped as he heard my voice.

Moving away from the overhang of ivy and things that grow on cliffs, and no longer hidden from view, I continued, 'I know these rocks.'

He looked at me, and then back at one of the stones which he had overturned.

'I could help!' I offered cunningly but he took no notice.

Another man rounded the corner, obviously having come down the steps from my father's shed. He wore gumboots and carried a bucket and briefcase. He was more observant than the man raking in the mud and saw me at once.

'What are you doing?' he asked fiercely with an English accent. 'Scram!'

Instead of pointing out that this was my wall, I jumped down and went to fetch my friends. Gwyneth and Eira were chatting with Dolly and all four of us stood the other side of the back door, looking through the cracks of the door frame and, as Dolly described it, 'spying'.

The first man turned over the stones with a stick, disturbing crabs and large cockroaches. We couldn't help laughing when he flinched every time the creatures ran across his boots. Finally, he looked up and we quietened down. He then sat uncomfortably on a rock to make notes.

The entire mudscape near the house was searched that evening. I asked my father what was going on.

'They're just looking to see what they can find.'

What sort of an answer was that?

'You mean worms stuck to the back of stones?' I asked, thinking of my prize pieces of crockery thrown away. 'I heard they're looking for the murder weapon.' I prompted. 'I think I saw it today,' I lied, to keep his attention.

'Yes?'

'But it was only a broken old kitchen knife.'

I invited him to join the spies behind the garden door, but he declined. I was surprised that such a fan of detective stories should refuse to view a real-life thriller. He seemed to prefer news relayed at the Brown's. Dolly arrived the next day full of her news. Her mother knew the landlady on the Grist who did occasional bed-and-breakfast and was putting up one of the London inspectors. She had vacated her king-size bed for him and was sleeping with her sister two doors down.

A few days later, the heron and Mother were stabbing, one with its beak and the other with a long fork, to spear flatfish hiding in the sand of the low river and the policemen were watching as we watched them. They had already cut their huge hands on the razor-shells, slipped on the seaweed hanging like a wet drape, and one careered across a virgin piece of mud to land on his bottom. It was high entertainment. Mother came back towards the garden door where we were hiding. The men looked up from their task as if a bird of paradise had been sighted. She swaggered, basket swinging with fish for dinner or lunch, the fork carried lightly, expecting silent applause, and when they looked down because their chief was there she looked up disappointed. They were crowding around one spot. That night Mum told me they had found a knife and the thrill of a thousand detectives shivered down my spine. When Dad came home, I was first to tell him the news but he'd heard it from the Brown's and Mother.

The prime suspect was busy as usual, mowing the lawn and doing any odd jobs around the house and garden. On the way to Granny's, I found him carrying a bucket of slops. After every meal Dolly emptied the leftovers into a bucket kept under the sink or, if it smelt, in the larder, a dank, dark room under the stairs and next to the kitchen. Booda put down the full bucket and mimed a pig. At first it looked like a dog as he wrinkled up his nose and made ears out of his hands placed either side of his head. When he added whiskers to the end of the ears I understood that he meant 'pig', and that the slops were destined for our pig, or more precisely the half-pig we had a stake in, fed for a year, then shared when it was killed, cured and distributed.

'Can I come to see the pig?' I asked, not forgetting to paint in the air the ears with the whiskery tufts, placing them on my head. Booda didn't seem to mind either way. As we were on the way to Granny, I remembered Booda might be a possible murderer. He looked the same as ever.

Granny was with her friend, the grey lady from Carmarthen, but looked delighted when she greeted me. To save her the business of slipping back and forth from Welsh to English to Welsh, I told them I was just going with Booda to feed the pig. A woman, dressed in fawn so close to her own skin colour you could hardly see the join, stood up to embrace me.

'It's Miss Davies,' said Granny. Then she went on in English for my sake about what a bright scholar I was, and such a loving grandchild. I beamed.

'It's all right, Gran,' I said. 'Must go.'

But Granny would not be stopped. 'Lovely manners she has, always polite, and thoughtful and generous to a fault . . . you can't say Caitlin hasn't brought her up properly.' Perhaps bringing me up properly was one of the few things about Mother that met Granny's approval. I couldn't bear it when Mother and Granny, the suns in my life, criticized each other. Always sensitive to my moods, Granny burst into Welsh.

Booda waited politely until Granny remembered to point to the scullery and he was allowed in to collect the other bucket. Taking the opportunity to escape, I followed him to make clear that I was going too. Booda seemed surprised when I started miming a pig snuffling and eating disgustingly from the slop buckets and then pointed to myself. He seemed to understand that I wanted to be there. I had my own set of gestures to communicate with Booda, including pointing, but I added new ones to extend his limited repertoire.

'You'll be coming back for a spot of lunch after,' said Granny as we closed the front door.

I accompanied Booda to the Cross House where he handed the Boat House and Pelican buckets to Phil Richards. We went together to visit the pig at the back of the pub. He was called Walter or Beery by my father, after the beer-slop sediment on which he was fed and the actor Walter Beery. Booda picked up the scratching stick propped on one side of the sty to scratch the hog's back. He grunted with pleasure as he devoured the slops, his head disappearing into the bucket. I tried translating the pig's name to Booda without success. He kept thinking I was offering him a beer as if I had the money to waste or was allowed to enter the pub with Booda and stand by the bar, barely able to see over the counter, the dead carcasses of pigs hanging from the rafters overhead.

Beery had been bought jointly by Phil Richards and my father from Billy Mayer, who lived in the Lakes District of Laugharne. Father and Phil tethered the pig by its hind leg while Phil's son, David, told them how to guide the pig to the pub. Billy Mayer couldn't give his expert advice because he was laughing so much. Whenever Dylan visited the Cross House Inn, he and Phil would lean on the sty and argue: 'My half is making better progress than yours.' When it came to slaughtering Beery, the fathers disappeared and left the butcher to do the killing and salting. The remains were hung up from the ceiling of the Cross House Inn, and the fug and smoke in the bar helped cure the pork. My father had grown fond of Beery but would soon eat his bacon with relish.

On the day I accompanied Booda with his pail of slops, I left the Cross House Inn to loiter at the bus stop on the Grist square. I was hoping to see friends, maybe at the sweet-shop, or even Dolly out shopping but only Mably appeared from nowhere, to disappear mysteriously again. He seemed to have more to do than I did.

I returned to the pub where Dad and Phil were conversing over the sty. There had been a drama: the chickens from next door had fluttered over the wall and Beery had eaten them. The owner was demanding compensation. 'I'll have to pay him back in pints,' said Phil dolefully.

'Have you seen Booda?' I asked meaningfully.

'He left the slops earlier,' said Dad, which I knew. 'Not that Beery will have much of an appetite,' he added.

'Granny says to keep out of Booda's way,' I said.

'Oh?' said Dad, looking at Phil in surprise. 'Go on home, now,' he said. I wasn't going to get much from them. Dolly would have to be happy with the chickens story.

'Have a biscuit and drink round the back before you go,' said Phil.

I looked at Dad to see if he'd let me. He smiled, 'There's a good girl.'

I still lingered and was rewarded with Phil and Dad taking up the subject nearest to my heart: the murder. Whatever they said I'd relay to Dolly and Booda. Dad noticed I was still there, told me to go to Granny's who was expecting me, then continued. He'd done his duty and so long as I didn't try to be part of the conversation he'd forget I was still around. I shrank to wraith size, standing back slightly, in an attempt to defy detection. I needed to gather information to relay something even more interesting to Dolly and the kitchen crowd who relied on me.

They took up the scratching stick absentmindedly, forgetting Beery was in disgrace. The pig grunted happily.

'Miss Elizabeth Thomas, didn't she live near your mother?' asked Phil. 'Is she taking precautions? My wife's locking every door in the pub and the customers have to ask for the key to go out the back.'

'My mother says he didn't do it . . . what would he do with all that money? . . . not the type . . . just because he was near the scene of the crime . . . others were round the Phillip's shop opposite the crime scene.'

'Thing is he knew Miss Thomas,' said Phil. She used to clean the church and, of course, Booda was employed as gravedigger.

'Yes, I thought of that one,' said Dad, 'but that would rule him out I'd say. She was very kind to him and brought him sandwiches from home.'

'Isn't it that most murderers already know the victim and that's how they gain access?' said Phil, who had suddenly become the expert.

Unfortunately, at that point, Phil turned to me and I knew my time was up so I disappeared to Phil's wife and her guaranteed welcome with a tumbler of lemonade.

With Granny and Miss Davies still talking in Welsh on my return to the Pelican, I went to the sideboard to take out some sewing. I found the basket with its padded interior for pins and needles, plastic divided boxes and a tiny silver thimble for me. Threading a large-eyed needle, I took two velvet squares and sewed them together with a stuffing of laddered stockings. It would become a buffer for dusting and polishing. Mother complained that Granny dusted everything in sight.

'Your father's coming to see me about now,' Granny announced and, as she heard the front door open, shouted out, 'Mr Morris.'

He was the lodger from upstairs and often seen given a helping hand to Granny. He put his head around the door.

'I'm just off to the Brown's,' he informed her.

'But Dylan will be here any minute,' she said, getting out Grandpa's whisky bottle which now lived in the sideboard cupboard.

'Yes,' agreed Mr Morris, 'I was hoping for a word. Try to cheer him up now his father's gone.'

Soon after, my father arrived, banging the front-door knocker. My father did not speak Welsh and Granny said in English, 'Hallo, dear'. He pecked her cheek, looking apologetic, perhaps because he had been drinking in the Cross House. Both men declined tea and Granny brought out two tumblers, pouring whisky from the bottle, and saying to Miss Davies, 'Just a nip – keeps the cold out.'

When Granny then returned to Welsh, my Dad seemed to follow the conversation, saying in English, 'That's very nice,' to Miss Davies who continued pleased in her first language. 'Oh really,' said Dad, 'I wasn't aware of that. Give him my best regards.' I had no idea what my father was referring to. He always seemed to follow the conversation when his relatives or Granny's friends visited but never spoke in Welsh. Wonderfully, they were speculating whether Booda had done it or not.

'I wonder whether they can bring a charge,' Mr Morris said, taking a draught from the tumbler. He continued, 'A deaf and dumb man would be unable to defend himself even through an advocate.'

'I should advise him to play on that,' added my father.

'What's the general view?' asked Granny.

Mr Morris looked surprised at Granny asking a question, and looked to my dad to answer. They were both silent, then Granny said, changing the subject, 'Do you want to go back with your father?' she asked as he stood up to go, gesturing to Mr Morris to join him. She couldn't call him Dad or Daddy because that's what she called Grandpa. Grandpa's son looked at me as if seeing me for the first time in his life. Generally, I was grateful he did not notice me much so that I could eavesdrop undisturbed.

'No, I think I'll stay if I may.' I was not going to miss lunch and pudding.

The lady from Carmarthen helped clear the table for lunch, braised lamb with leeks and potatoes followed by egg custard.

'You'll be staying to lunch, won't you?' she was asked.

'Will it stretch?'

'Aeron can have scrambled egg if necessary. She doesn't mind.'

I only just managed to conceal my thoughts on the subject.

'Yes, that's all right,' I said to the fawn lady who had a little more colour now in her cheeks, perhaps with the thought of lunch.

Granny returned to the Booda story. She seemed tolerant.

'He couldn't hurt a fly, poor thing. Very nice he is to me when he comes to collect the slops and help me with the heavy things,' she said as we laid the table. 'But you keep your distance,' she said to me, 'just in case.'

'Do you share the pig, too?' I asked.

'Oh yes, we've got a quarter. Mr Richards arranged it . . . it's not the same pig as your father's.' I now understood where all the hams downstairs were coming from. 'We always used to have a whole pig but there's only two of us now.' Then, remembering Grandpa was no longer with us, she changed this to, 'There's only me now. I'll have some egg custard for it today, I shouldn't wonder, and yesterday's rice pudding. I'll be throwing away the old one.' She looked at Miss Davies, 'Unless you'd like it cold before you go.'

'I'm not fussy,' she said.

Was she saying yes or no? Welsh people talked in such an indirect way, Mother said. Mother called a spade a spade, though that was an expression never used in our household. Miss Davies had brought vegetables, broad beans and cabbages from her smallholding and I was asked to take them into the larder. 'I can sell what I like at the market but always I keep some back for friends.'

'Oh Aeron,' exclaimed Granny, 'you've dropped your sewing in the tea now . . .' It was very confusing with vegetables, tea and lunch preparations all together and everyone speaking Welsh. And now Granny was cross with me. She looked worried and upset. I stopped my snuffling and hid in her arms to console us both.

'There, there,' said Miss Davies, sympathetically. 'I'll take you to Carmarthen market, one day, and you can help me on the stall,' she consoled.

'She had a tidy bit of money in the house,' said Granny, following another train of thought. Then, correcting herself, continued in Welsh.

I knew 'she' was the murder victim who reportedly kept money in the house, tempting thieves and, as it turned out, would-be killers. Money was so scarce that before the war Laugharnies bought and sold houses on a bartering system, exchanging labour for goods and commodities and even property. Granny said that Richard Lewis, or Dicky the Milk, had told her about the bartering. They were more sophisticated in Swansea and Carmarthen, she said to the grey lady. She turned to me.

'Imagine, Aeron, you'd do a bit of gardening or shopping in exchange for a lunch.'

I was thinking that the huge sum of £200 might have seemed worth killing for . . . in Laugharne.

On my way home I found Booda peeing against the cliffwalk wall. Dolly had sworn he did it on purpose when she was passing but I wasn't sure whether she imagined this or not. But there he was peeing, then pulling his flies together, looking over the wall at the panorama, and probably acting like a murderer. The next day he was charged in his proper name: George Roberts.

Soon, the reports came in and circulated round the small town like wildfire. The courtroom dramas were relayed and repeated a hundred times. Booda was on trial at the St Clears Court, only four or five miles up the road, then sent to a bigger court in Cardiff. The pathologist's report was published in the *Carmarthen Journal* and instantly read, discussed and chewed over by a hundred locals, making everyone fearful and locking their doors in the day. Some had locks installed on doors left open for years. Mother disdained all such panicked reactions, saying she'd stayed at her post (that is to say, the bar counter) during every air-raid and would be ready for anything the enemy might throw at her. I pitied anyone who tried and imagined them receiving a beating with the hairbrush they'd never forget.

After a while without incident, people began to wonder whether Booda could have inflicted such dreadful injuries on Miss Elizabeth Thomas. She had been battered round the head with her own wooden draft excluder and stabbed seven times in the chest and back. The stabbing appealed in particular to us children and we used our penknives to brandish about threateningly, picking up driftwood to represent the draught excluder in our version of 'Murder'. There were endless permutations of the game. One was running away and hiding but sticking out a weapon to suggest where you might be until some-one with knife or wood found you. You battled it out until one fell down, vanquished and dead. I was sure Booda would have enjoyed joining our games. We wondered if he would ever return and when he did we were delighted.

Booda Returns

T hat day, after I had collected the bread from the baker's in King Street, I remember slicing the white loaf warm from the oven into doorsteps and trying to cut round the hole I'd eaten on the way home. We were all there when Booda turned up. We had heard of his acquittal and that the court case was cancelled indefinitely because of communication problems and lack of evidence but it was still a surprise to see him. He was greeted enthusiastically and offered a cup of tea by Dolly and a slice of bread and salty Welsh butter by me. I went to find the Robertson strawberry jam from the larder. He nodded towards the teapot which stewed all day on the Aga. Mother said our stove was a Rayburn but everyone called their stoves 'Agas'. Dolly insisted on brewing a fresh cup and filled the kettle. Booda sat down and we waited. Dolly took a pudding basin and mixed flour, fat and currants for welsh-cakes. Booda looked on greedily. He had a sweet tooth. As Dolly took the wooden spoon to mix the lard and flour, he began to tell us.

First, he painted the courtroom scene with gestures, grunts and grimaces. He played the idiot (tapping his forehead) and mimed an inability to understand or make himself understood even with a deaf interpreter. He had never been taught sign language. Then the scene widened to include all the participants: the judge with his gavel seen through Booda banging a spoon, the perplexed judge wrinkling his brow and the resigned solicitors shrugging their shoulders, demonstrated by Booda swinging his imaginary gown, thumbs under the flaps. Finally, he gave us the moment when he was freed, pointing to the door and to himself. He showed his pleasure in his freedom by simulating laughter.

'He's laughing because he made fools of them,' said Dolly.

'No, he's only showing how pleased he is not to go to prison.'

'Yes, he's pleased he's got away with it, for sure,' said Dolly. 'I heard he made out he was "twp",' assuming a silly expression and tapping her forehead. 'He wouldn't speak to anyone, not even to his own defence counsel, pretending he couldn't understand anything,' she claimed.

As he knew so little of the official deaf language Booda would quickly learn everyone's style of mime at the Boat House. It was amazing to me that Desmond, the least extrovert of all the children, managed 'to speak' so well with Booda.

I was right to trust Booda with our own safety. They eventually found another prime suspect, Ronald Harries of Pendine, and it was sustained that his motive was financial gain. Supposedly, he had hoped to steal the money hidden under the mattress. He had been disturbed by someone knocking loudly at the door and had escaped the back way before getting his hands on the loot. The case against Booda collapsed. Also, by the time Ronald was first suspected as Miss Elizabeth Thomas' possible murderer (the open verdict remained), he had gone on to kill two people that he called 'Auntie' and 'Uncle', though not relatives, for the same motive and in much the same manner.

'Speak no evil, hear no evil, like the monkey,' said Mother in answer to my demands to know more about Booda's court appearances. I stored away this new expression for future use. Was it one of Mother's 'takes' on clichés? 'That's the game he played, I expect. I don't blame the poor bugger. I'm glad he's back. Your father wants to go to Llanybri and maybe Booda will take him across at high tide with the Cuckoo. His uncle used to take us both ways in the ferry boat.'

I knew that and I knew you rang the bell the other side when you wanted to come back. One of my school friends and I had visited the bell-house at low tide. No one had bothered to demolish it when the last ferryman died.

'Shall I go and tell Booda?' I found him walking up his own cliff path, and he was told three of us were going to Llanybri. He was more interested in the boat than the occupants.

'What? In the Cuckoo?' He mimed Colm's boat and shook his head. 'Too light and dangerous.' I knew he was comparing it to the ferry boat that was long gone. He followed me to the house and without a second's hesitation, agreed to take us, touching his cap and rubbing his fingers together to show it would cost. Mother said he'd have to wait to be paid.

At full tide, we stood at the harbour entrance ready to go. When I clambered on board, there was consternation. 'But Dolly said she can't look after me.' I claimed, no one believing me. I whined and made horrible, suffering grimaces in my father's direction. He was weaker than Mother and we were soon on our way, Booda rowing towards the bell-house. The water lapped and circled around us.

Booda was right. The Cuckoo was too light a vessel for Laugharne at full tide. I flitted between Mum and Dad at either end until they made me sit on the boards, flicked by water from the oars. But they couldn't stop me talking.

'How's Booda going to hear when we want to come back? There's no bell and he can't hear anyway.'

'We'll send out a distress signal,' said Dad, 'a flair or a rocket.'

'We can borrow it from the Establishment,' I agreed.

'We'll come back by road,' said Mum prosaically. 'Tudor will send someone out to collect us.'

Booda wanted to say something but couldn't with the oars in his hands. To my great delight, I was allowed to hold them while he asked the same question. Dad tried to gesture that we would return by car after the family visit to Llanybri but Booda thought he meant to add an outboard motor to the Cuckoo for the return.

'No, no,' I intervened, dropping an oar which Booda caught as the tide threatened to carry it away. I gestured to include us all, then mimed Tudor Williams, pulling up the gaiters that Tudor wore, then sat down on the rowing seat to demonstrate driving a car in the manner of Toady screaming round the bends. Booda understood and laughed, mimicking a mad driver with oars . . . not that the Williamses drove particularly fast.

Another Tour

When 20 April arrived, father left on his third tour of America. Caitlin did not accompany him. This time, perhaps she really thought they'd go for a sunny holiday in the bleak months, when Laugharne was dark on my walk to school and the light faded early. Her resentment at his flight to the United States, where she said to Brinnin he was looking for 'flattery, idleness and infidelity', justified her own growing promiscuity. If Mother had been another woman she would have followed my father on his third and fourth tours, without making scenes, disputing his stories and interrupting his anecdotes to adoring post-performance audiences.

On the other hand, if she had been another woman he would not have married her. Years later, at a pleasant lunch organized by the publishers Dent's, a friendly Pamela Hansford Johnson, still shaken by a serious operation, told me she could never have married Dylan. She wanted to reform his drinking habits, a mistake never made by Mother, and he was having none of it.

Although everyone in the town told us to give a wide berth to Johnny, when we heard his dog was dying we ignored the warnings. With everyone warning us against him, we knew that he relied on his German shepherd, an ancient dog that resided outside much of the time, for companionship.

'He messes when he comes indoors,' explained Johnny, 'and he's got the shed. I put newspaper down when he comes in for a warm.'

The day we went to visit the ailing dog, there were four of us for safety. But Johnny's only thoughts were for his dog.

'How's Larry?' we asked of the dog, named after Larry Adler. The dog lay, wheezing and whimpering from time to time, on yesterday's *Daily Express*, in a corner.

'Can't afford the vet,' he said. 'Anyway, he's a goner. He'll stay indoors now till he goes. Can't see no more,' said Johnny.

The dog flapped its tail, slowly recognizing me. When he could still walk, I often met him and his master on the cliffwalk. Lately, he had become so thin you could count the ribs through his coarse coat which was bald in patches.

'I'll have to get Mr Dark to shoot him one of these days,' Johnny said, beginning to weep.

AERONWY THOMAS

'Let's go and buy some sweets,' suggested Eira. We bicycled down the hill, propped our bikes against the stone cross on the Grist and bought 'black jacks', small hard toffees in wrappers, with dark flakes that broke off in your mouth like slate. We sucked until our tongues turned black.

'Who's got the blackest tongue?' said Eira.

'I have,' I claimed, sticking it out.

'No you haven't, just the biggest mouth,' she retorted.

Eira and I shared our sweets, two for a penny. We put our ha'pennies together to buy arrowroot, a short stubby twig with a distinctive taste. I couldn't decide whether I liked it or not. I'd try again and see. We forgot dog and master, until the next time.

We bicycled to the Boat House when I mentioned Dolly was doing some baking. We pulled Clive along too when we discovered him by the biking shed.

'I was hoping to borrow Welly's bike,' he said, referring to Llewelyn.

We persuaded him to sit in the kitchen but he was uncomfortable so close to Dolly and Booda as he felt, quite rightly, that they did not approve of our friendship or his family. When Clive went outside for a moment, Dolly quickly mimed to Booda a larger version of Clive, his father, and put manacles on his wrists. When Booda did not quite catch on, thinking Clive was in trouble, Dolly pretended to fall off a bike. Clive's dad was often seen weaving along on his bike at pub closing time and sometimes falling off when he negotiated corners. Clive was treated to guilty smiles all round on his return.

He refused the offer of a second jam tart and on his dignity said

196

he had to go. I joined him on the cliffwalk where he was muttering, 'They were talking about me. I know it.'

To put him in a better mood, I said he could kiss me. Without enthusiasm, he pecked me on the lips not even holding my shoulders to steady us, then put his arm round my shoulders in case anyone from the Boat House passed by to see us and we walked slowly to the town.

I asked him about the new bike he was getting.

'Oh, it's only Him-Next-Door's that's giving it to me. His son's too grown and he said he'll put the brakes right first. He's leaving me to look after the tyres. They'll be seeing it soon enough,' he said, pointing over the stone wall to the Boat House to indicate the gang.

Dad in America

This time he only stayed for six weeks. My dad started his affair with Liz Reitell after a reading of *Under Milk Wood* at Fogg Museum, Harvard, on 3 May 1953 and progressed after the same reading with a cast of actors on 14–28 May at the Poetry Center, New York (where she worked as an assistant to Brinnin). In addition, Father accepted a commission to write a libretto for Stravinsky. On his return, he wrote to Llewelyn telling him about his latest broken arm. He had fallen over a suitcase in a New York hotel bedroom.

Dad didn't write to Colm and me but mentioned us in letters. Promising presents, a 'leather travelling-bag for Welly to go with his travelling rug'. He adds, 'And whatever I can think of for darling Colm and dear Aeron.' Welly was the family's name. I noticed the 'dear' for

*Aeron (aged about ten) and Colm;
Aeron, Llewelyn and Colm; Aeron
(aged about twelve) and Colm with
car.* (Photos courtesy of
Rene Harding).

Aeron – perhaps being ten years old now I didn't need a 'darling'.

Of course, he was also writing his love letters to my mother: 'I love you, Caitlin Macnamara, I love and love you. People here know that, although I would never say it. They can see the love for you around me; they can know I'm blessed. I'm damned if I'm blessed, but all the eyes of the strangers can see that I am in love with you. I love you . . .' Back in London, though, he was also writing letters to Liz Reitell who had instructions to address her letters to his London club. 'Liz love, I miss you terribly much,' he wrote in a much cooler tone.

He returned the day after the Coronation of 2 June, when the streets were littered with the debris of parties. Almost immediately, he and Caitlin went to a three-day house party at Margaret Taylor's. He was in a state of exhaustion and dying to return to Laugharne but Mother, starved of fun, was determined to stay. He was delighted to get back to Laugharne.

His health had visibly deteriorated in those few weeks away and, as he worked on his talk about the Eisteddfod, I could hear his racking cough. Every morning, he had a prolonged coughing attack which subsided eventually, allowing him to wheeze downstairs, his lungs sounding like the bellows we used to encourage our open fires. The coughing was nothing new but it seemed worse than before.

I told him about Johnny and his ancient dog.

'What's he been doing with you children?' he demanded. He knew all about Johnny's reputation. I got annoyed that Dad did not understand that the dying dog occupied all of Johnny's thoughts and emotions. It took me time to explain the new situation and Dad seemed to understand. Then he said, 'Keep away from the old lecher.'

Dad was shocked that I had dared to be with him without adults present. I had to explain and justify even further, saying that Mr Dark might have to shoot the dog. I saw a flicker of compassion on Dad's face but he must have told my mother because I was not there when Larry finally gave up the ghost. Eira told me she'd visited with her mother after the event and Johnny was sitting unmoving and almost unseeing for the entire time. Unbelievably for me, Johnny was walking along the cliffwalk without his dog within the month. I had imagined him pining away at home, going the way his dog went.

Following this episode, my parents decided I was to leave home for the Arts Educational School, a theatrical boarding school in Tring, something already discussed between them. I hated the prospect of being banished from Laugharne. It was agreed that the new school term in September would be the best time.

Despite the routine worries about present and future debts, my father took up his work again, revising and completing *Under Milk Wood*, the 'Elegy' for his father and broadcasts. New Directions published *The Colour of Saying*, an anthology of favourite poems he had read in America.

We continued to pursue our reading as we hadn't finished the stories in *The Wind in the Willows* and managed to finish it before he returned to America once more. We no longer discussed the demerits of Toad. We both agreed he was a hothead and rebel but couldn't help admiring his panache. He'd take the trouble to dress the part – goggles, gaiters and huge overcoat for his racing days in oversize motorcars. Very satisfactory. So Dad and I loved Toad and didn't like the weasels destroying his home while in prison, though he deserved it!

Our new discussions centred on where we'd choose to live if we were an animal from the book. I liked the idea of living by the Cherwell, the Oxford river, where I could make a comfortable burrow under one of the willows which dipped green tendrils like hands into the water. I think Dad also liked somewhere near the river, too. But he tactfully said he'd make himself a snug near Badger in the middle of the Wild Wood and visit us all on the river bank daily.

As we came towards the end, the remaining pages seemed so few that I spun out our sessions with even more talk. Did Dad think that Mole, Rat and Badger, not forgetting Toad, were clever to outwit the weasels and their gun-toting soldiers, the ferrets and stoats, to reclaim Toad Hall? By wielding cutlasses and relying on the element of surprise did he think they could have thought of something else to trick them? Dad prosaically countered that it worked, didn't it, and to remember Badger's big frame and savage teeth. Then we put our minds to other subterfuges they could have used.

'Pity there wasn't a stretch of water that took them directly to the house,' opined Dad.

Our fancies took flight, imagining the animals in frog-suits frightening the assembled crowd in the dining room by throwing around fireworks when they arrived.

Instead of remembering a secret passage from the river bank to the inside of the house in order to surprise the weasels, who were banqueting and carousing, and rout them, Toady and friends could have enlisted Badger and all the river folk to dress like stoats and ferrets. We thought up other stratagems but concluded the author had the best ending. I liked the idea of the secret passage as it reminded me of the tunnel under the flagstones by the Boat House front door.

My own subterfuge to extend the book had some success but eventually we turned the last page and in desperation I took down the books he had brought from America to start when we returned from a planned family trip.

A Trip North

We finished the book just before leaving for Llangollen in North Wales. Dad had been commissioned to write about the International Eisteddfod and Llangollen by the BBC producer, Aneirin Talfan Davies, so in July 1953 my parents and I set off by train to North Wales. We stayed at a family boarding-house in a street of terraced houses.

The marquee of the Eisteddfod was huge and a tunnel of canvas led to the main arena where the choirs competed, to be judged, so far as I could see, by men covered from head to floor in white drapes. My father said they were called druids. We waited for twenty minutes or so, shepherded here and there by nervous, sweating men in suits, my father smoking one Woodbine after another. A suited man told him to stub out his cigarette when a young, pretty woman appeared in a floral dress, high heels and hat, a leather handbag across her arm. She was steered to our side. She talked to someone before us, then came towards my parents with a huge smile, as if we were the people she was most pleased to see.

My father was nervous, and bereft of his comforting cigarette, but rallied himself to answer the Queen's questions, of which there were about three.

'Was he enjoying the Eisteddfod?' she asked, pronouncing Eisteddfod correctly.

He mumbled, 'Yes, very colourful.'

She then became more personal, 'My mother, the Queen Mother, asked me to send her warm regards to you.' This was not a question and Dad thanked her with some animation, mumbling something to the effect that he returned the kind regards and remembrance.

'I hear you are representing the BBC this year?' she both stated and asked.

'Yes,' said Dad and told her briefly of the commissioned broadcast.

The suited men were nudging her away as it looked as if she'd overstayed. She acknowledged my existence, with a kind smile and nod towards me, to remain vivid in my memory. My hair had been brushed to crying point and Mother insisted I wear my new dress, a pretty sprigged yellow, made to order from Carmarthen market material. Mother looked like Rita Hayworth with stacked heels and a suit with a polka-dot silk blouse. Dad wore a respectable suit of tweed which he found too hot for the day.

My father seemed awed, even stunned, by the occasion until he was safely back in the pub, with me hidden in a corner. He was told 'no children' by the man behind the bar, who had spied me by then, and jogged back into reality. The bar man relented when he heard about our encounter with royalty and gave me a lemonade. Dad relaxed at the bar with Aneirin Talfan Davies, telling him about his last meeting with royalty, when the Queen Mother met him for the second time and remembered his name. He said how pretty and young the new Queen Elizabeth seemed and 'unspoilt', I think he said.

'Rather an unfortunate plummy accent,' countered Mother.

Mother and I wandered round to see the dancers in the streets before returning to collect my father, still chatting at the bar.

After this interlude, life at Laugharne continued. Dad's health was a constant source of comment at the Brown's where twice he had suffered a blackout. After a walk, Phil Richards told Mother and me that he'd been called the week before to collect Dylan with the car from Carmarthen cinema where he had lost consciousness and for a while did not know where he was.

'I don't like it,' said Phil. 'He's taking a risk every time he goes to the States. He travels around on his own and, say, he blacks out on the train and nobody knows who he is or what he's saying. Mind you, he doesn't talk when he's ill, he just goes silent. It's terrible to see.'

Mother said Dylan would be going back to New York over her dead body.

In August, he interrupted his writing to appear on television, his first solo appearance, which was destroyed after use. He was to read 'The Outing', sometimes called 'The Story'. Mother and I watched him on the Brown's television set and Mum made unkind comments because he had failed to memorize all the text. The box at the Brown's was one of the early televisions with a 9-inch screen and sepia colours, but of course it was thrilling to us.

Television was in its infancy and there was no studio near so Dylan travelled to St Asaph Cathedral in Denbighshire where he was filmed in the library of a clergyman by one of television's most experienced cameramen, a young man called David Gardner. On visiting the Boat House later, Gardner found Mother at her most charming, and incurred my father's jealousy. A little later, perhaps not so soon as Mother might have wished, they began an affair. He was in awe of her, a superior, glamorous creature in his eyes, though in need of support after the death.

A journalist visited us in the last late summer of my father's life and witnessed one fight started by my mother. When asked about his plans to return to the States, my father told him they were well advanced, only the dates had to be agreed. Mother went berserk, landing a swipe on Dylan's head. The onlooker looked appalled and tried to calm the situation.

'You bloody bastard,' she said to my father, who tried to ignore her. 'You said that you'd only return for Stravinsky, taking the family.'

'All right, all right,' he said, shielding his head uselessly as Mother punched him in the gut.

This signalled a proper fight with the two of them locked in a deadly embrace, Mother continuing to rain blows on this back and Dad defending his front by squeezing Mother uncomfortably.

Another fight of this type also occurred that last late summer. Vernon and Gwen Watkins came to visit and, as the scuffle began, I ran away screaming, or so Gwen told me later but I have no recollection of that particular episode. The Watkins left earlier than anticipated.

What Mother was most angry about in those last few months was my father's insistence on returning to the United States. She said he was encouraged by John Malcolm Brinnin and Rollie McKenna, who came to Laugharne in September. Brinnin denied this, saying he encouraged my father to stay at home and concentrate on his writing, particularly when he saw his poor health. He claims that it was with great reluctance that he set up further readings. My father insisted on going. Perhaps he thought he could escape from his problems and himself by embarking on another tiring tour, promising Mother she could join him in California when he started work on the Stravinsky libretto, and perhaps stay there with the family if he got a post at a local university, a place in the sun.

Mother's discontent became apparent to all of us. It was a day in the summer holidays when Llewelyn was missing, probably with his older friends, and Mother was nowhere to be seen. Dolly said Mother had gone walking; she had heard Mably barking excitedly, being told to stay. It was a shock to have been forgotten and I fought tears as I thought about the betrayal. Dabbing my cheeks, I followed the usual route, running, hoping to find her and after a while saw her figure in the distance striding purposefully along. Behind me, and at a distance, Mably followed knowing he was not wanted. She didn't hear me shouting so I ran even faster. She turned a corner by the farm and I stopped to catch my breath as I knew the next part of the walk was uphill.

Though anxious, I couldn't help noticing how green everything still looked: the leaves on the trees were out, the fields were extra lush with new grass and, as I panted up the hill, the tall damp hedgerows were awash with foxgloves. Taking another breather near the top, I realized with an awful sinking feeling that Mother wasn't there in the distance. She wasn't following the usual route. Frantically, I ran along another road which eventually turned into the main road on to the hill down to the church. I found her by the church gate, sitting.

'Oh,' she said, not realizing I'd followed her. 'What are you doing here?'

Sweaty and flustered I didn't tell her at first but eventually recriminated her.

'Oh, yes, I forgot,' she said by way of apology. In a change of mood she suggested having a lemonade at the Cross House.

Soon, we were friends again. Today she didn't disappear with Crossmouse but remained with me – more subdued than usual. All this talk about America was upsetting us all.

Last Tour

I cannot remember whether my father or I left first, he for the United States and I for school, but I suppose it must have been me because he did not leave until October 1953, arriving by plane on 19 October to settle into the Chelsea Hotel for his remaining twenty-one days.

He had visited my new school and had expressed his satisfaction at the grand building previously owned by the Rothschild family. The rooms had walls covered in rich red brocade and had been adapted for ballet, with barres along the sides and a large mirror at the narrow end. In the gardens, Dad attempted to perform the cygnets' dance from *Swan Lake*, making a jolly tune of the sublime music. The grounds consisted of a vast lawn and meadows covered by yellow cowslips in the spring.

Father was impressed, as I was, by the Elizabethan gardens, formal hedging and lawns, where the pupils performed Shakespeare and the classics, weather permitting. He couldn't resist miming a line or two when our guide turned her back.

My father seemed excited by the school even without seeing the pupils in action, practising their pliés and arabesques. He and I were not to know that ballet was not my forte. He wrote me a lively letter full of references to the ballet steps I was supposedly mastering and I felt that I could be a golden child, rivalling my brother Colm who was prettier and with a sweeter disposition.

Just over a month after starting school, I was told my father had died.

Mother told me that my father's departure was not a happy time in spite of friends – the Lockes, Margaret Taylor and Douglas Cleverdon – rallying round to see him off at Victoria and supporting her after-wards. In New York he struggled through the rehearsals of *Under Milk Wood*, adding last-minute revisions, raising himself for the actual performances with the cast at the Poetry Center. Sometimes he was helped on and off stage by Liz Reitell.

He was drinking heavily and was administered injections of morphine and cortisone. He managed a handful of engagements before he collapsed and was taken as an emergency to St Vincent's hospital in New York. My mother received the news in a telegram while she was attending a BBC programme at the Laugharne Memorial Hall. She did not want to face the consequences immediately and she told me how she went on to dance somewhere for the rest of the evening.

'I was just trying to blot it all out,' she explained to me, 'but drink and enjoying myself didn't work for long . . .' In her heart of hearts she knew it was the end but hoped that her instincts were wrong.

In a hastily arranged flight, she arrived at New York to find her husband under an oxygen tent. It is well-documented how she tried to light a cigarette and with her enforced removal she lost all control. She was restrained and taken to a psychiatric ward, where she was inexplicably denied water which she kept demanding and was told that Dylan was dead before he finally succumbed on 9 November 1953. As I write, I am still outraged at the picture of Mother in intolerable pain being treated so insensitively.

She knew my father's body had to be returned to Laugharne for burial, not least for Granny Thomas' sake, and she accompanied the body back. The morticians had transformed him into a tailor's dummy with a new American-style executive suit. She told me much later that his hands were still the same: narrow like fish fins 'like yours but useless'. Mother was not sure for a long time whether her last damning letter to my father was ever received. It was a relief, she said, when she learnt that the letter in which she informed him their marriage was over, without knowing about his latest infidelity, was never delivered to him. When she wrote the letter she was devoured by anger and pain and unsure whether the break would be permanent.

The funeral in Laugharne, which took place on 25 November, has been recounted from various viewpoints. The body was exhibited in a coffin at the Pelican, with a friend remarking, 'He'd never have been seen dead in that tie,' and all his close friends from London and Swansea drinking tea with Granny. Booda played

Dylan's funeral.

Master of Ceremonies in the front room with the open casket displayed for all the mourners. He ushered reluctant viewers to the coffin, encouraging them to move in close for a better view and even to touch the body in a farewell gesture. He was inordinately proud of the role assigned him by Granny and subsequently played out the scene to Dolly and companions in the Boat House kitchen. When I first saw Booda, during my first holiday from school, in full mime and grimace, I needed Dolly to interpret. She had popped her head in at the Pelican to see for herself. Fascinating as it was, I soon got fed up with Booda repeating the same scenes over and over. The reception, he told us in mime, was held in the Brown's as the numbers were too great for the Pelican and where a beer was available.

Llewelyn complained that no one visited him to tell him of Father's death, nor invited him to the funeral. He had to hear the news from his headmaster.

Granny was telling everyone that Dylan's health had never been good and no one had the heart to quote the medical verdict of death by alcoholic poisoning, couched in the ambiguous words, 'insult to the brain'. The controversies about drugs were still a whisper amongst the friends and acquaintances.

At the grave, her arm held firmly at the elbow, Mother said she thought briefly of throwing herself after the coffin. Considering the passionate nature of their relationship I don't think my father would have expected less. Mother was nearly forty, her dead husband thirty-nine years old.

Around this time, Aunt Nicolette came to my school. I was looking forward to an afternoon in the village and being treated by her to a hotel meal. While we were walking down the drive away from the school, with me still in my new uniform and grey hat, she told me. 'Something has happened to your father,' she said, by way of introduction.

I sensed immediately something awful.

'Is he still in New York or is he in Laugharne?' I asked, not wanting to know the truth. He might just be ill.

'He became very ill and was rushed to a hospital called St Vincent's in New York.' Normally, my aunt was very direct. I realized he must be dead or dying for all this preamble. 'Unfortunately, he has died,' she said, finally coming to the point. I couldn't think of anything to say and concentrated on settling my stomach, which was heaving uncontrollably, with an act of will.

'Are you going to be sick?' asked Nicolette. She knew the signs as she had often had to stop the car on long journeys. It was too embarrassing, I thought. Now, I felt faint. Nicolette knew these signs, too. 'Now sit down and put your head between your legs.'

After a minute or so, I could lift my head without feeling dizzy. Then we talked about other things.

The teachers were worried and asked the pupils to check whether I was crying at night. No, they reported, no sign of grieving. No one could understand that I carried on my life at school as if nothing had happened. Writing about my father's death is cathartic, though all my activity on his behalf, during most of my life, has been a form of reconciliation to his death. Nicolette continued to behave as a good friend when Mother went away to Italy, collecting, delivering and letting me stay with her family at Carlyle Square.

My brother Llewelyn had more difficulties and dealt with them differently. His memory of not being informed personally of his father's death fuelled his feelings of alienation from his parents. When it came for him to choose a resting-place, having been informed in August 2000 he was suffering from terminal lung cancer, he chose Ellingham Church graveyard with the graves of the Macnamaras. Now I'm older myself I wonder why he hung on to the huge resentment against his negligent parents, which was so immensely destructive to himself. Our parents were largely unaware of the lifelong effect of not listening to his wishes, and I wish he could have found his 'poor peace' with them before his death. His stoicism and courage in the face of cancer was learned during those school years of silent suffering spent at Magdalen, he claimed.

In a weak moment he stated that God (of whose existence he gave little or no credence earlier) would look after him in the next world. I wonder if, in this supposed second Eden, he could ever be reconciled to his mother whom he considered, 'cruel, feckless and thoughtless'. In Mother's defence, I think looking after my father took a great deal of her thoughts and energy. When her husband died, she was bereft, with moments of despair when she looked at the empty bed, describing her attempts to forget with other men, drinking and unruly behaviour which did not give her any lasting satisfaction.

After the funeral, Mother was left to decide what to do with the children, the Boat House and Granny Thomas. Margaret offered to sell Mother the house but the £1,400 was not there. Mother considered taking Colm and Granny to California to stay with Ruth Witt-Diamant but this came to nothing and she stayed on in Laugharne for a year or two before leaving to live permanently in Italy.

So many times my parents dreamed of moving to Spain, Italy or California, a place in the sun. In reality, my father preferred the damp and drizzle, the constantly shifting weather of coastal Wales, the landscape of his writing and living.

I stayed at my dance and drama school in Hertfordshire, taking spring walks by myself on the hill covered with cowslips, escaping via the 'ha-ha' fence bordering the grounds until I was caught. There was no punishment as I was considered in bereavement and a special case.

Holidays were spent in Chelsea with Aunt Nicolette and her welcoming boys, Esmond and Prosper, as well as the painter Anthony Devas, who was kind to me. In longer breaks from school, I was put on the train from Paddington to Carmarthen, my mother collecting me when she was still living in Laugharne before her permanent exodus to Italy, the country she yearned for while still married. She took Colm with her to Italy, and Llewelyn and I visited her there in the longer holidays.

In 1955, I returned to Laugharne to see Granny, to see the Boat House, to see Dolly, to see the Brown's and the people I remembered. Granny said she was never lonely as so many people loved Dylan and would visit her to talk about him. She had moved into the Boat House which made her feel close to her boy and from the balcony she could see where she was born, just over the brow of the hill. I understood what she meant. In the poem 'In Country Sleep', he warned me against death, 'the Thief as meek as the dew', but here despite his early death he still lived in his poems about Laugharne: 'Over Sir John's Hill', 'Poem in October' and 'Poem on his Birthday', in particular. Granny no longer loved me in the same way, I felt, and looked sadly at me when she thought I wasn't looking, seeing Dylan once again in my features which so resembled his.

I made an excuse to get away and went paddling near the lichened rock; the tide came in and I scrambled up the steps to his shed to look over the cliff.

Appendix

Later Than Laugharne
by Aeronwy Thomas

Herons, mussel pools, gulls and pipers,
encircle our 'house on stilts high among
beaks and palavers of birds'. Cormorants
scud and gulls glide in my memory.
The stones, washed by the tide, which I
would turn looking for blue and white,
or floral pieces of china for our crockery
houses . . . And the fish my mother would
catch and throw back into the swirling
waters of the estuary all around us . . .
I remember them well.
. . . And high tide covering our back garden
through a hole in the stone wall which
embraced our home. The tide carrying our
makeshift boats on its back, pieces of lumber,
an old zinc bath, and I can still recall
the envy I felt when they bought my brother
a boat called The Cuckoo . . .
The names come tumbling back –
. . . And I remember the hole in the wall was
called grandly by all, The Harbour.
. . . And who could forget sliding down the

mud banks at low tide into the rivulets
left by the receding water, or running along
the cliffwalk and stirring up a din outside
the shed that was my father's writing den.
The memories race back –
. . . And the thrill of peeping through
the keyhole (I was always the most naughty)
to see my father writing his poems about
gulls, hills and cormorants on estuaries
which he saw through his wide-vista window,
as he sat, bent, writing in crabbed letters,
pressing against the hard surface of the
kitchen table that was his desk . . .
We were poor those days –
Though I can't remember being poor
in Laugharne, those balmy,
never-to-be-forgotten days,
green and golden . . .

Herons, gulls and pipers still encircle
our house on stilts,
and the cormorants still scud and glide
in my memory . . .

Acknowledgements

A s this book took ten years to write from start to finish (including the expert editing), I have to acknowledge and thank a number of people for talking to me or for the material in their books. Author Sally Fiber's book, *The Fitzroy, The Autobiography of a London Tavern* (London 1995) was useful but visits to the establishment where her father reigned behind the bar when Dylan and fellow artists and performers of the BBC met in the 1930s were even more illuminating and enjoyable.

Lorraine Scofield, manager of the Boat House and author of an excellent tourist guide about our one-time home, was always willing to answer questions and check the text for geographical or any other inaccuracies.

The ex-emeritus professor of Birkbeck College, Barbara Hardy, and author of an excellent memoir, *Swansea Girl*, was one of the people who never lost her faith in the content of my own memories, loving the characters I remembered when living in the Boat House, encouraging me and making suggestions for improvements, particularly in style.

One of the first people I showed an early version of the memoir were friends Reg Evans and his wife Eileen. Generously, they let me have the use of photos in their possession, many of them unpublished.

Dylan Thomas has many biographies written about him which I used for date checking and chronology, and I also asked for personal help with some vexing details from the past. I'd like to thank in particular Paul Ferris, Andrew Lycett, D.N. Thomas and Hilary Laurie.

And to finish my acknowledgements I must remember Leo Hollis, who with great patience edited my rough prose into a smooth read, the copy-editor Howard Watson and my agent, Pat Schooling.